SPITTING ON A SOLDIER'S GRAVE

SPITTING ON A SOLDIER'S GRAVE

Court Martialed after death,
the story of the forgotten Irish and British soldiers

ROBERT WIDDERS

Matador
5 Weir Road
Kibworth Beauchamp
Leicester LE8 0LQ, UK
Tel: (+44) 116 279 2299
Fax: (+44) 116 279 2277
Email: books@troubador.co.uk
Web: www.troubador.co.uk/matador

ISBN 978 1848764 996

British Library Cataloguing in Publication Data.
A catalogue record for this book is available from the British Library.

Typeset in 11pt Aldine BT by Troubador Publishing Ltd, Leicester, UK

Matador is an imprint of Troubador Publishing Ltd

Printed in Great Britain by the MPG Books Group, Bodmin and King's Lynn

To Corporal Lou Hauser RAuxAF

in pace, ut sapiens, aptarit idonea bello

Thank you

Contents

Author's Note

Nothing in this book is intended as a criticism, direct or implied, of the many Irish soldiers who felt that their duty during World War II lay in continued service within the Irish Army.

A number of databases were used and cross-referenced throughout my research. The smallest of these holds nearly 5,000 names; the largest, the Commonwealth War Graves Commission register, consists of nearly 1.75 million names. These databases were compiled from original wartime and post-war typescript and handwritten records. Inevitably, with data on such a vast scale, errors creep in. To further complicate matters, in certain cases, men falsified personal details such as names, date of birth, and place of origin. Any errors or omissions that are brought to the attention of the publishers/author will be rectified in future editions.

The term "Irish Army" refers to the Irish Defence Force. During World War II, most people referred to it simply as the Army, or the Irish Army. The names "Eire," "Ireland," and the "Irish Free State" refer to the Republic of Ireland. These names have been used interchangeably throughout this book, as they generally were during the period in question.

In Part II, I have written about a representative sample of Irish Army deserters who died fighting in World War II and were later court-martialled by the Irish government. Usually, very little information survived the death of an individual soldier on the battlefield during this time. I have used official records and contemporary accounts, such as battalion war diaries and memoirs, to tell their stories as best I can. These men fought and died in every theatre of war: on land, at sea, and in the air. However, this book doesn't pretend to be a comprehensive account of World War II. So, whilst I have included some background information about the war, readers may wish to consult other works to put the material in context.

Preface

It took me a long time to settle down after my service with the Royal Air Force during the First Gulf War in 1991. We'd completed our mission and liberated Kuwait from Saddam Hussein and the Iraqi army of occupation. But, perhaps inevitably, life felt rather tame after that. I left the military and drifted around, doing everything from studying history at university to being a Ranger in Africa and a Brussels sprout sorter in Cork. Eventually, ill health forced me to settle down in one place and try to come to terms with my chequered past. That was when I wrote my own military memoir, *A Few Deeds Short of a Hero*, about my service in all three branches of the British armed forces: Army, Royal Navy, and RAF.

A few months after my memoirs were published, I happened upon an out-of-date book about Irish history, languishing on the shelves of a charity bookshop on Thomas Street, in Limerick. In it was a footnote, just a few lines—a dismissive, almost contemptuous, reference to deserters from the Irish army during World War II.

Intrigued, I did a little research. As it turns out, over

70,000 men from (Southern) Ireland joined the British armed forces during World War II. Thousands of these men were deserters from the Irish Army. They left the safety of neutral Ireland to fight Nazism and liberate the many nations of Hitler's new Europe.

After the war, the Irish government court-martialled these men en masse and *in absentia*. Under Fianna Fáil Taoiseach (or prime minister) Eamon de Valera, the men were formally dismissed from the Irish Army and stripped of all pay and pension rights. The government also circulated a list of 4,983 names and addresses, entitled, the "List of personnel of the Defence Forces dismissed for desertion in time of National Emergency." The aim was to prevent those men from finding work by banning them for seven years from any employment paid by State or public funds.

This seemed just the topic I was looking for to resume my attempt at an academic career. I decided to write a standard doctoral thesis, though I knew it would likely gather dust on the shelves of academia along with other specialised texts. Then I spoke to Richard Fellows.

Richard, who lives in Dublin, contacted me in June 2009, in response to a request for help with my research published in an Irish newspaper. He struck me as a very modest sort of person, one who spoke quietly and matter-of-factly about his past. During World War II, Richard told me, he'd joined the Royal Air Force and volunteered to serve as aircrew. When we finished talking, I thanked him.

He paused. Then: "Not a bother. Phone me if you need any more information."

"No," I replied, "I meant thank you for what you did for us all during the war. Thank you for the courage and self-sacrifice that you and your pals showed when you stood up against fascism and Nazism."

Richard went silent again for a few moments. Then he said quietly, "No one's ever said thank you to me before."

Of course, his generation, the 'war' generation, never asked for thanks. They just got on with life. But I couldn't help thinking of Richard as I continued filling my manuscript with references to other authors in my attempt to be scholarly.

A few days later, at 8:30 on a Saturday morning, the phone rang. *Who the hell is calling me at this time?* I thought, falling out of bed and picking up the phone. A raised female voice said, "I'm Kathy Ferguson. I'm phoning about your ad in the paper . . . I want to tell you a few things." Almost shouting, she demanded, "Do you know what happened in the war?"

I listened, trying to make sense of her narrative, conscious of the raw emotion in her voice. When she finished, I thanked her for calling. Then I sat on the edge of the bed, thinking. Surely the State didn't imprison infants—even in 1948? Surely children weren't kidnapped off the streets of Ireland? Could the authorities have really condemned Kathy, then a child, to years of abuse in industrial schools for being the illegitimate daughter of an Irishman who'd served with the British Army during the war?

I admit to, initially, being a little incredulous. Then I started making inquiries. I read victims' accounts. I checked facts on the Internet. I read the Ryan Report. It was all far worse than I could have imagined. I felt physically sick as I learned about the litany of physical and sexual abuse committed against children in the Irish industrial schools.

A few weeks later, I got my third shock, when I went to visit Con Murphy, who had deserted the Irish Army to serve in the RAF in World War II. Con had responded to a letter I had published in the *Irish Independent*.

"Come on in," he said, answering my knock on the door of his neat little cottage in County Cork. He led me inside, and then sat down in a high-backed chair in the front room. When he leaned toward me to start talking, he burst into a fit of coughing. After he recovered, I prompted him with a few questions. Then I listened, enthralled, as he told me about his experiences during the war.

His final comment, about his wartime service, was typical of all the men I spoke with: "I didn't do anything special at all in the war," he said, with genuine modesty. Of course, volunteering to serve in a global life and death struggle, and defending democracy against the Nazis, seemed pretty special to *me*. But I kept my thoughts to myself, and we finished the interview.

"So, when's this book comin' out?" he asked me.

"Oh, I don't know for sure. It could be a year or two," I said, conscious that there was a lot of work left to do.

Con looked at me. "That's a shame," he said, without a trace of self-pity. "I was hoping to see it before I die."

"I'll do my best, mate," I said, smiling weakly.

It all seemed clear then. I went home that evening and deleted thousands of words of pseudo-academic drivel from my computer; let the academics argue over *exactly* how many Irish deserters died fighting with the British Army whilst defending democracy. I would write as a soldier, speaking on behalf of other soldiers. Their stories deserve to be told *now*, whilst there are still a few left alive to hear some long overdue and inadequate words of thanks.

The Irish people deserve to know the truth about their World War II heroes. And they deserve to know about the 133 pages of printed injustice called the "List of personnel of the Defence Forces dismissed for desertion in time of National Emergency".

The List was condemned in the Dail in 1945 by the opposition party, Fine Gael. The party's deputy leader, Dr. Thomas F. O'Higgins, described it as ". . . brutal, unchristian and inhuman, stimulated by malice, seething with hatred, and oozing with venom".

But the List was even more mean-spirited and vindictive than the opposition realised: Hundreds of men on the List had died long before they were court-martialled. Men like Joseph Mullally, from Westmeath, would never cheat the dole queue and get a job with the council. He died on D-Day, 6 June 1944, fighting the Nazis on the beaches of Normandy—a year before his name was added to the List. And Stephen McManus, from Sligo, would never get a job on the railway or with the Electricity Supply Board. Along with thousands of his comrades, he suffered torture and starvation whilst being worked to death in a Japanese prisoner of war camp.

This book tells the story of these brave men and many others like them.

PART I

Chapter 1

Ireland and a World Heading Into War

The first fascist dictator to emerge on the world stage was Italy's Benito Mussolini. Mussolini took power in 1922, and in 1935 Italy flexed its muscles with an invasion of Ethiopia. Failing to defeat the Ethiopian tribesmen by conventional military means, Italy turned to illegal chemical warfare. Its main weapons were mustard gas and phosgene, outlawed under the Geneva Convention of 1925. These weapons rained from the sky, causing horrendous casualties amongst soldiers and civilians alike, and the Ethiopians had no defence against them. Then, in a callous foreshadowing of things to come, Italy bombed the International Red Cross hospitals in Ethiopia that were treating the casualties. Predictably, in 1936, Italy won this war and "Il Duce" celebrated with a grand victory parade in Rome.

But Italian fascists were really just amateurs in the field of barbarity compared to their soon-to-be ally, Japan. Strictly speaking, Japan wasn't a fascist country. But during the 1930s, under the influence of the Japanese Army, it developed its own particular brand of fascist-style totalitarianism. This was expressed, at its most brutal, through the Japanese invasion of Manchuria, a region of northeast China. The sickening apogee of the military campaign was the seizure of the city of Nanking.

In December 1937, the Japanese Army defeated the numerically superior, but militarily inferior, Chinese forces defending Nanking. Then they committed a series of atrocities on a scale that would be difficult to believe, were it not so well filmed and documented. Literally thousands of civilians – elderly people, women, and children – were machine-gunned. Women were raped; none were spared, not even the youngest children. Pregnant women, too, were often raped and then had their bellies slit open with a bayonet, the living foetus wrenched out. People were burnt alive; people were buried alive. During this six-week orgy of death, 300,000 people (about half of the city's population) were murdered.

The third and senior member of the fascist triumvirate was Nazi Germany, under Chancellor Adolf Hitler. This Rome-Berlin-Tokyo axis, known more simply as the Axis, was formally recognised by a treaty in September 1940. And the Axis truly was, in reality and not rhetoric, an Axis of evil.

Germany had annexed Austria in March 1938. In September 1938, Hitler demanded the Sudetenland from Czechoslovakia. Emboldened by success, he then invaded and subjugated the rest of Czechoslovakia in March 1939.

Germany's territorial and moral position, spelled out in Hitler's *Mein Kampf*, was now blindingly clear in practice. The policy of appeasement, expressed by decent, well-meaning men like British Prime Minister Neville Chamberlain, had failed to inhibit Nazi Germany's territorial ambitions in Europe. Hitler, though, was an admirer of the British Empire and claimed, plausibly, to have no territorial ambitions against Britain. So a pragmatic approach of disengagement and neutrality to European affairs remained a possibility for Britain.

Meanwhile, the next target on the *Führer's* list was Poland. France already had a defence treaty with Poland, but Britain didn't, so Britain entered into an agreement to defend Poland. This brought Britain into a war that would eventually cost hundreds of thousands of British and Commonwealth lives, destroy the British economy, hasten the end of its Empire, and bring about its demise as a world power.

On 1 September 1939 the German Army marched into Poland, destroying the Polish Army in only two weeks. Great Britain honoured its commitment to defend Polish sovereignty and demanded that Germany give a commitment to withdraw. Three days later, British Prime Minister Neville Chamberlain broadcasted to the nation on the BBC. He announced, in sombre tones, "I have to tell you now, that no such undertaking has been received, and that consequently this country is at war with Germany."

Six years later, in May 1945, the war in Europe ended

with Hitler's personal *Götterdämmerung* in the blazing ruins of Germany. Then, in August 1945, the twin mushroom clouds of Hiroshima and Nagasaki announced the final defeat of Germany's fascist ally, Japan.

And during those six years, the world experienced the worst and bloodiest war in human history, a worldwide conflagration that claimed over 55 million lives and left countless other millions wounded and traumatised.

When war broke out in Europe, the Irish Army found itself seriously under-manned and woefully ill-equipped. Throughout the 1920s and 1930s, the army had been organised, re-organised, and constantly underfunded, a situation not unfamiliar to the armed forces of other democratic countries at the time. Now it lacked not just the essentials of modern warfare – such as aeroplanes, artillery, tanks and anti-aircraft guns – but even sufficient stocks of small arms ammunition. And when the Army mobilised, in September 1939, it soon partly de-mobilised due to budgetary restrictions.

Like all armies, the Irish Army had a duty to prepare for every conceivable eventuality, no matter how unlikely. So plans were drawn up to defend against a British invasion, in case a pre-emptive attack was launched to deny the German army the chance to use Eire as a springboard for an invasion of Britain. However, despite some rhetorical sabre rattling from British wartime Prime Minister Winston Churchill, this was never seriously contemplated by Britain. And throughout the war, relations between the Irish Army and the British armed forces were generally excellent, with British instructors helping to train the Irish Army and Air Force.

Meanwhile, Germany prepared itself for the occupation and government of Ireland. A Gauleiter, or Nazi provincial governor, was to be stationed in Dublin – an extremely unpleasant prospect, as the inhabitants of countries like Czechoslovakia had already discovered. Germany contemplated using Ireland as a base to strangle the flow of oil and essential raw materials entering Britain via the Atlantic, and as a launching pad for an invasion of England. Fortunately, Hitler lacked the maritime resources to defeat the Royal Navy at sea and transport a large invasion force to Ireland.

It was equally fortunate that the German *Luftwaffe* failed to destroy the Royal Air Force during the Battle of Britain in 1940. Without air superiority, Germany was unable to launch an invasion of England directly across the English Channel. If it had, Eire's fate would have been sealed. At best, like Vichy France, Ireland would have been governed by German-approved fascist ministers, forced to export Irish Jews to the gas chambers of Auschwitz and Treblinka, to exterminate physically handicapped babies, and to adopt all the other disgusting characteristics of Hitler's Third Reich.

Unable to invade England, Hitler turned his attentions to the east. In June 1941, the German army, then the toughest and most ruthlessly efficient combat force ever seen in the modern era, invaded the Soviet Union with over three million men. They inflicted more than thirteen million casualties on the Soviet armies and killed another seven million civilians before the end of the war. Had Hitler had been able to land a German force of this calibre on Irish soil, Eire would have been doomed, despite the undoubted courage and determination of the, at most, 37,000 soldiers of the Irish Army.

Ireland remained neutral throughout World War II. Both America and Great Britain were highly critical of this. But Ireland probably had little real choice at the time. This was a country that had not long won its independence, and had then fought a painful and divisive civil war. And joining the Allies would have alienated a significant part of the population, and probably led to widespread civil unrest.

But whilst the Irish state considered neutrality to be the only option, on an individual basis, many Irish citizens clearly felt differently. Around 70,000 Irish citizens joined the British armed forces during World War II. And these men and women were, de facto, blood guarantors of Eire's neutrality – as were the Irish army deserters who would later be placed on the List.

Chapter 2

The King's Shilling: Recruiting for the British Army

Irishmen had been joining the British Army for generations, and this didn't change after independence. But opinion within Ireland on the morality of recruiting for (or joining) the British Army varied widely. Throughout the 1930s, groups and individuals with strong nationalist views complained about it. At the same time, Irish men and women who retained pro-British sympathies continued to help men who wanted to travel to Northern Ireland or England to enlist.

Unemployment and poverty was widespread in 1930s Ireland. Young men in Dublin often went to places like the Soldiers' and Sailors' Help Society meeting rooms, or the Soldiers' Home in Parkgate Street, to get warm, meet friends, and have a cup of tea. Like the British Legion, these organisations had worthwhile charitable aims, helping ex-servicemen who were suffering from the effects of poverty or homelessness. They also served as social centres for former soldiers and sailors and their families, and were seen as "British" institutions.

The Irish government had no objection to the charitable activities at these places, but was concerned about their alleged role as unofficial recruiting centres. A report by the Irish Department of Justice stated, "Recruiting for the British Army is being carried out in Dublin by ... persons of independent means with pronounced imperialistic views."

The report cited Mrs. Crawford, the Lady Superintendent at the Sailors' Home, and Miss Sandes, the manager, as examples. The two women mingled with the young men, discussing the men's problems and telling them about the advantages of joining the British Army. If a man said he wanted to join the British Army, he might be cared for at the Sailors' Home for a few days before being lent the money to travel to Liverpool or Belfast. Or he might be sent to see Mr. Peare, a consulting engineer, at Mr. Peare's office in Grafton Street for the same purpose.

There were many other people helping men to travel to England to enlist, and undoubtedly they had pro-British leanings. But they also saw their actions as altruistic. In helping young men join the British Army, they were helping them escape unemployment and poverty. Also, men with strong nationalist feelings were unlikely to visit charities and institutions associated with Britain. Conversely, men with a family tradition of service in the British Army, and pro-British sympathies, were more likely to visit, sometimes with the intention of getting help to travel to a recruiting office. So the men being helped to enlist were those who had expressed a wish to join the British Army, after having visited a place known to offer assistance.

The Irish government recognised that the thin line between responding to requests for help and actively encouraging enlistment was not being crossed. So government officials saw little point, and perhaps less likelihood of success, in legal intervention. But social and economic imperatives also influenced Irish thinking, as shown in a letter from the Department of the President of the Irish Free State, to the Minister for External Affairs: " ... in the present circumstances, my view is that these boys would be better off *everyway* [sic] in the British Army, than hanging around corners here."

An Irish Ministry of Justice memorandum put matters even more starkly: "If young men ... find an outlet for their energies in the British Army, I do not feel that we should, in the present economic conditions, endeavour to prevent them. *They are better in the British Army than in our gaols.*[sic]."

But, with the outbreak of a world war and Ireland's stated policy of neutrality, there were concerns voiced within the Cabinet – fuelled by vociferous complaints from Nationalists – about continued recruiting for the British Army.

However, it wasn't illegal for Irish citizens to join the armed forces of another country, though it *was* illegal, under Section 58 of the Defence Forces Act (1940), for anyone from another state to induce or persuade Irish citizens (within Eire) to join the armed forces of that state. The UK government possibly saw this as a grey area in relation to the British Army, as Eire was still nominally a member of the Commonwealth. But there was no doubt about the Irish government's view of the matter. The Cabinet Committee on Emergency Problems took seriously any allegations that Irish citizens were being assisted, or induced, to go to Britain to enlist. And investigations were launched to determine the validity of such claims.

There were two main concerns, regarding recruitment and retention, for the Irish Army: After the initial patriotic surge of volunteers in the summer of 1940, the government struggled, for the remainder of the Emergency, to find enough men willing to serve in the Irish Army. Within the Army, there was also deep concern about the rate of desertion. A secret report prepared in 1941 by the Irish Army stated that, "... the numbers of men deserting [that year] rose in an alarming manner." In August of that year alone, 450 men deserted. This was a massive number for an army whose nominal strength was only 40,000. The army responded by stationing Garda (police) and military police to monitor army barracks and border crossing points. But, whilst the level of desertion lessened under these measures, a steady flow of men continued to make it across the border to Northern Ireland.

Many Irish soldiers were deserting to join the British forces. In most cases, they did so without help or inducement. But the Irish government thought these men must be getting assistance from an organization like the British Legion. So they put together a sting operation led by Private Roy O'Callaghan (Corps of Engineers), and assisted by Corporal William Power. At first sight, it seems odd that the ostensibly junior of the two men, Private O'Callaghan, should be in charge of the operation and should write the formal report. But Irish intelligence services were probably the driving force to this and later operations, acting, in this case, as *agents provocateurs*.

So, on 1 March 1941, O'Callaghan and Power went to the British Legion Club in Baggot Street, Dublin. They asked for advice and pretended that they wanted to join the RAF. A Legion official, Mr. Hyland, said that if they brought in two references, they would be given a letter (a character reference) that would take them over the border to Northern Ireland. Then O'Callaghan allegedly revealed that he and Power were both already in the Irish Army.

Mr. Hyland replied, "You are now treading on very dangerous ground, but if I were in your position I would know what to do." He didn't suggest that they to desert, nor did he offer any inducement. He advised them to see Major Tynan, at the British Legion office at St. Stephen's Green, Dublin. He knew that Tynan, a retired British Army officer, would be able to help them to travel up north to enlist.

Three days later, O'Callaghan and Power called at the

Legion office and asked to speak to Major Tynan. Again, the two men pretended that they wanted to join the RAF. After asking a few questions, Tynan told them to get references from a responsible person and their previous employer. At this stage, O'Callaghan claims he told Tynan that he and Power were serving in the Irish Army, which would obviously make acquiring an employer's reference problematic. Then, according to O'Callaghan's account of the conversation, Tynan repeated his offer to provide a reference, knowing that the men were serving Irish soldiers.

Major Tynan, a former officer decorated for bravery during World War I, later denied that this was the case. But regardless of which account is accurate, there was no personal gain for Tynan in helping Irishmen to join the Allies. People like him saw an occupied Europe groaning under the heel of the Nazi jackboot; in helping men to fight with the British Army, they were contributing to the war against Nazism.

The following day, O'Callaghan produced an authentic reference from a priest and a faked employer's reference from the G.S.R. Railways. In return, he was given a letter addressed "To Whom It May Concern". It stated that:

"The above [Roy O'Callaghan] is a very good type of man and has expressed a desire to join the British Army. I can recommend him as he can produce Testimonials as to character."

The Department of Defence later produced a report recognising that in this, and a number of similar cases, participants had been careful to avoid any breach of the Defence Forces Act. No one had actually been *persuaded* to enlist in the British Army; they were merely given character references. And as these reference letters weren't essential for enlistment anyway, the British Legion (and others) wasn't considered to be actively recruiting for the British Forces. The reference would, though, help the bearer pass through the control points on the Northern Ireland side of the border.

Nonetheless, a detective sergeant, from the special section of the Garda detective branch at Dublin Castle, visited Major Tynan. He warned Tynan to stop his activities, especially regarding deserters from the Irish Defence Forces. Major Tynan replied that he didn't give out vouchers or travel passes, or anything else except character references. Then he strenuously denied knowingly helping members of the Defence Forces to join the British Army, and asked to see evidence of the allegations.

A visit to Mr. Hyland saw similar accusations and denials. So did visits to Mr. Connolly at the tax office in O'Connell Street, and Dr. Maunsell in Dún Laoghaire, both of whom had been accused of similar practices. In each case, the Garda's message was the same: The Irish government takes a serious view of your activities; stop, or action will be taken. In answer, all three men denied encouraging anyone to join the British Army and argued that it was unfair to try to prevent them from giving character reference letters. But, regardless of any limitations placed on the supposed activities of the British Legion, potential recruits continued to travel in significant numbers across the border to join the British Forces.

Chapter 3

Phil Farrington and the Road to Belsen

Phil Farrington lives in a neat little terraced house in Dublin, only a few streets away from the home he left over half a century ago when he joined the Irish Army. When we met, he looked frail and tired as he told me about his experiences in World War II. He spoke quietly, hoarsely, and I strained forward in my seat to listen. I asked him why he'd deserted from the Irish Army. He said, "To start with, I was looking for adventure."

"What did you feel about Hitler and Nazism?" I asked.

Phil hesitated, clearly struggling with memories long buried. He smiled, briefly. But it was a smile that didn't reach his eyes. I felt awkward, not knowing quite what to say. So I changed the subject and asked him how he'd got to England to enlist.

"I told my mother and grandmother that I was going," he explained. "I needed six shillings and sixpence for the train. Then when I got on the train [to Northern Ireland] I recognised most of the men on it."

Phil arrived in Belfast and went to the British Army recruiting office.

"They asked me my name and where I lived. I joined the Royal Sussex Regiment [infantry]." He added, "I wanted to have a go …"

As a volunteer, Phil could choose which trade or regiment to join, subject to vacancies. He could have opted for a non-combatant branch and become a driver or storeman, or whatever. But, like the overwhelming majority of Irish volunteers, he chose a combat role in the infantry. And one of the ironies of military life is that the infantry, which usually has the highest death rate in war, at least in the Army, has the lowest rate of pay.

Like thousands of others, Phil took the well-trodden path to Liverpool en route to an infantry training depot. "They could tell the men who were trained," Phil said. "There were a lot of other Irish Army deserters in the Royal Sussex Regiment. And they treated us very well there. After training, I was sent to my regiment, which was in Brighton. Then I was stationed in Guildford.

"I got seven days leave and took the boat to Dún Laoghaire. When I got off the boat, a man said, 'I know you – I'll have to take you in.' Then I said, 'I don't know what you're talking about.' But he took me to a barracks anyway. I'd used my own name – I didn't think they'd nab me."

"I was put in the Guardroom at Griffith Barracks. The guard corporal said to me, 'I'll have yer thrashed to death.' But I was sent by train, along with a lot of other deserters, to [a military prison in] Cork. I knew a good many of the men on the train. Some got three months. Some got six months or even a year."

The prison, or detention centre, in Cork had all the hallmarks of a brutal regime totally out of control. There appears to have been little supervision from higher authority. At best, this might be seen as negligent. At worst, it was intentional. Perhaps the punitive regime of illegal punishments and starvation was unofficially allowed, to deter others from deserting from the Irish Army. One sergeant told Phil that the Minister of Defence had ordered that "the prisoners should be shown no mercy," and that the minister "didn't care what happened to them." Of course, this may have simply been harsh rhetoric made up by a jailor. But given the reality of the conditions, it has an air of plausibility.

According to Phil, there were hundreds of deserters in the prison. Starvation and physical brutality was endemic.

"We were never allowed to speak to each other, and we got no food," Phil told me. "In the morning, we got a little bit of bread and butter. At the end of the day, we had a little bit of bread and maybe an egg, an' that was your lot until the next morning. Sometime you might get a little bit of fish. But it was more bones than fish. Though I was so hungry, I'd chew the bones and eat them. Sometimes they used to throw the food at us, just like we were animals. The men who worked there wasn't the best, some of them."

"We were in jail through the winter. It was freezing cold without any bedding or heating. And once a week we'd all be hosed down with cold water. Sometimes we'd have to stand to attention for hours in the freezin' cold, in a pair of thin fatigues [overalls]. It was bad, all right."

Then Phil described some of the other punishments.

"We were made to work all day scrubbing concrete floors. If you slowed down, you'd get a kicking. There were lots of beatings," he revealed. "One fella' was beaten so bad that he was taken to hospital and we never saw him again. It got so bad that some men tried to commit suicide."

"There was a sergeant in charge of us. He said, 'If you want to cut your throat, then go ahead and do so, or if you want to swallow the buttons on your coat and choke you can do that'. They didn't care what happened to us."

"Some days, we had to run around a [prison] yard for hours, carrying bricks on our backs in a haversack. One little man I knew took it really hard. He came from near me, and he missed his wife and little kids. The jailors made him run up and down, whilst they threw lumps of turf at him until he collapsed."

After release from the military prison, Phil was so ill and traumatised that he was admitted to a civilian hospital for two weeks. After that, he was sent back to his Irish Army battalion. Then he deserted again and returned to England.

"I couldn't re-join the Sussex Regiment, so I went into the Pioneer Corp. I was in London during the bombing [air-raids], and some of our lads were wounded. After D-Day, we ended up in Germany. But we were lucky," he said. "We weren't in the worst of the action. Then at the end of the war, we went to [liberate] a concentration camp. My pal said, 'My God, look at that.' We were trying to give [the survivors] water and talk to them, God love them. We were there for a good long time doing various jobs."

This was Belsen concentration camp, which was liberated by the British 11th Armoured Division on Sunday, 15 April 1945. Unprepared for the horrors that awaited them, shocked soldiers did their best to keep the camp's inmates alive. Phil found it understandably difficult to articulate his feelings about the concentration camp. But he wasn't the only Irishman at the liberation of Belsen. Father Morrison, an Irish priest serving with the British Army, also witnessed its horrors. In a letter written to his sister, he described the camp in words that are all the more powerful and telling for their simplicity:

"… I forgot to mention that I am in Belsen concentration camp. There has been quite a lot about it recently on the BBC … though I expect the photos would not be published in Irish papers. I have seen some of the photos which appeared in English papers, but they do not reproduce anything like the real horror of the place. When we got here there were some thousands of naked dead bodies lying about the place. In one pile alone there were over a thousand women's bodies and it was quite common to see people crawl on their hands and knees because they were too weak to walk, whilst others just dropped to the ground and remained there. There were sixty thousand people crowded into an area of much less than a square mile. Some of the huts in which they lived had bunks. It was not uncommon to find three people in one bunk – one or more of whom were dead. Huts which could accommodate thirty were made to hold five to seven hundred.

The death rate for the first few days we were here must have been nearly a thousand a day. Typhus was raging, but starvation accounted for most deaths.

So far I have buried over fifteen thousand and I have not been able to attend all funerals, as I considered the dying more important than the dead. Those fifteen thousand did not take up much of my time as ten graves held up to five thousand bodies each."

After the war, Phil was de-mobilised and returned to Ireland. I asked him if he suffered any prejudice or ill treatment because of having served with the British Army.

"I tried to keep it quiet," he said, "but I was warned not to visit certain areas – or they'll have you."

Finally, I asked Phil if he felt proud of his wartime service.

"Yes, I do in ways," he said. "But I don't like to brag about these things."

Quiet and modest, like many of his comrades, Phil's final words were for his friends, who came back from the war traumatised by their experiences.

"When they came back after the war," he said, "a lot of them turned to drink. It was the things they'd seen …"

Chapter 4

Industrial Schools: Sins of the Fathers?

Father Morrison, whose letter is quoted in the previous chapter, is a shining example of the priesthood at its finest. For weeks on end, he selflessly tended the sick. He gave the sacraments to hundreds of dying people every day at Belsen concentration camp. He risked his life, surrounded by thousands of people dying from typhus, typhoid, tuberculosis, and the effects of starvation. This is the power of the church as it should be.

It's a sad irony that, at the same time, the Irish government and the religious orders were running their own camps in Ireland. These industrial schools were set up to provide 'care' for thousands of children whom the Irish State arrested on the flimsiest of pretexts and then handed over to the religious orders. "It was a system designed ... to let the religious, who controlled and ran the institutions for the State, beat faith into the children while at the same time they were starved, treated cruelly, and physically and sexually abused."[1]

In effect, the Irish State ran a system of religious controlled labour camps that required an ongoing supply of children. The industrial schools were paid per head – so if they ran out of children, they would lose their income. During World War II, one of the measures taken to maintain 'supplies' was the passage of the 1941 Children's Act. The Act allowed the State to imprison a child in an industrial school when one of the parents was absent from the family home. It also allowed the State to deny petitions from, and on behalf of, the absent parent.

Of course, fathers were often absent then in Irish families. There was a high rate of unemployment, and Irishmen frequently had to travel to England to find work in industry or agriculture. The Act doesn't generally seem to have been applied in those instances. But it was used in the case of families where the father had joined the British Army. And it had especially severe effects on Irish Army deserters who joined the British Army. Because these men were unable to safely return home before the war ended, their children were even more likely to be imprisoned.

The fact that aspects of the 1941 Act were unconstitutional was ignored, despite challenges in the Dail. The motivation was punitive and cynical: The Irish government was able to punish the deserters by harming their children, and, at the same time, gain from it financially.

The Irish government profited from taking Family

1 The Irish Gulag, Bruce Arnold, Gill & McMillan 2009.

Allowance payments from children. The Family Allowances, funded by the UK, were meant to be paid *directly* to the family concerned, and used to buy food and clothing for soldiers' children. The funds were intended to alleviate hardship and were an enlightened measure designed to promote child welfare.

But the Irish government lobbied the British government to have the payment of Family Allowances, to which married Irish soldiers in the British Army were entitled, paid directly to the Irish state. In effect, this helped finance the incarceration of the soldiers' children in the industrial schools. This would have been bad enough, even if the children had been decently cared for. But this was not the case. At their worst, the conditions under which the children were imprisoned echoed those of the Nazi concentration camps or the Stalinist Gulag: Children were tried in court and imprisoned without any real representation or right of appeal. In some industrial schools, children's names were replaced by numbers. Former child inmates recall beatings with rubber truncheons – a favoured weapon of the Nazi Gestapo: "The beatings of the other little children were terrible to witness … they were helpless and would huddle together and be lashed … then the lay sisters or nuns would leave …"[2]

One of the worst camps/schools was Artane, in Dublin. The 'Christian' Brothers running the school were, reputedly, fanatically republican and venomously anti-English. It would not have been a good place for the

2 Arnold, The Irish Gulag

child of an Irishman fighting with the British Army to end up. Of course, it wasn't a great place for any of its victims, even those convicted *just* for the 'crime' of illegitimacy.

There were no limits and no controls over the physical punishments inflicted on the children. Some children were sexually abused. Nearly all the children were psychologically traumatised by their treatment. Allegations of disappearances and unmarked graves have been made, which is not surprising considering that malnutrition, bordering on starvation, was commonplace. Children were sometimes rented out to farmers and used as agricultural slave labour. Medical care was often rudimentary, and sometimes totally nonexistent. Scabies and chilblains were commonplace, and former child prisoners' accounts of the so-called treatment for it are heartrending: "The nuns had a way of treating both ailments. They took stiff-bristled floor scrubbing brushes and scrubbed the children's hands until they screamed. Their flesh was often red and bleeding."[3]

Kathy Ferguson, the lady who telephoned me early that Saturday morning, was one of the victims of the industrial school system. She was taken from Main Street, Killaloe, and put on trial for illegitimacy. But she didn't manage to put up much of a defence: Kathy was three years old when she was sentenced in court.

Kathy was incarcerated in Ennis industrial school, and other institutions, for the crime of illegitimacy. But she

1 The Irish Gulag, Bruce Arnold, Gill & McMillan 2009.

was also punished for another sin: Her father fought with the British army during World War II.

Kathy Ferguson spoke not just for herself when she told me, "The life we had in these places was a childhood of abuse. It seems that the crime we committed was that a lot were born illegitimate. Our country, parents, and any relations we had were lost to us forever. A lot of parents, like my father, or the man that I was told was my father, fought [for Britain] in the last war. Did you know that this was another reason why we were incarcerated into these hellholes?"

It's very difficult to know what to say, or how to help, when confronted with accounts as traumatic as Kathy's. It's half a century too late to remind the religious orders who victimised the children in their care, of the words of Psalm 79:8: *Do not hold against us the sins of the fathers; may your mercy come quickly to meet us, for we are in desperate need.* They would not have understood the words. And it's beyond the ability of this author to understand how Church and State could have conspired together to treat children so appallingly for ideology and financial gain.

Chapter 5

The Money Myth: Why Did They Join?

There is no question that poverty has, historically, influenced many men to enlist in the military. Harsh economic conditions in the 1930s, for instance, induced men into uniform in many countries around the world. But this motivation has been far too readily ascribed to Irishmen who served during World War II.

Even respected, and much quoted, academic enquiries, such as the University of Cork's Volunteers Project, appear ready to just take this explanation for granted. When interviewing World War II veterans in the early 1990s, interviewers asked closed and leading questions, such as, "Why did you volunteer for the British Army – was it for adventure or money?"

The almost automatic assumption of pecuniary motives is widespread and long standing. For instance, in June 1945, Patrick Shannon and Patrick Kehoe were tried by military court-martial for desertion. It was a high-profile case that seems to have contributed much to the belief that deserters joined the British forces for financial reasons.

Kehoe joined the Irish Army in 1940 at the age of 15 and served with the 22nd Infantry Battalion. He deserted and joined the Royal Air Force when he was 18, and later volunteered for service with Bomber Command. Given the appalling casualty rate in Bomber Command, this was a brave action indeed. In March 1945, after 22 operational missions over Germany, Kehoe was shot down, captured by the Germans, and held as a prisoner of war for six weeks.

After his release from the prisoner of war camp, Kehoe travelled home to Ireland and was arrested whilst visiting his mother in Dundalk. When asked by his defending officer, Captain Cowan, why he deserted, Kehoe's answer was straightforward: "To get a crack at Germany because of what my relatives had gone through at the hands of the Nazis."[4]

This probably wasn't surprising, given that Kehoe's mother was English and his Irish father was still serving with the British Army. But Captain Cowan made a moral force argument in Kehoe's defence. He pointed out that the popular meaning of desertion was "leaving a post of danger for a post of safety". But Kehoe had done just the opposite. He'd left the safety of the Irish Army for a post of great personal danger fighting Nazism. And this, Cowan pointed out, "in any civilised country, was not a

4 Irish Times. 13th June 1945

case for punishment at all". The court, however, did not accept this argument.

Cowan then went on to defend Patrick Shannon. Shannon had joined the Irish Army's 2nd Infantry Battalion in June 1940. A year later, he deserted and joined the British Army. Shannon fought in North Africa and Sicily, including the Anzio beachhead. He continued in combat with the British Army, fighting up through Italy until he was captured in Florence. When Italy surrendered, he was released and eventually flown home on compassionate grounds to visit his dying mother. Coincidentally, Shannon's mother also lived in Dundalk, and he was arrested there by the military police before he could see her. In trial, Captain Cowan, defending, asked Shannon why he'd deserted. Shannon replied that he couldn't support his dependent mother on 14 shillings a week from the Irish Army. This answer was readily accepted by the court and the press: Perhaps too readily.

Of course, Shannon could have stood in front of the men who had the authority to imprison him and said, "I deserted to free Europe from the Nazis." He could have said, "I fought for freedom and democracy," to his former comrades who didn't. But he was not likely to argue with the court and say such things, even if that was what he felt.

Any man who has served in the ranks for four years learns how to look after himself. When standing before a court-martial, soldiers (as this author can personally testify) usually tell authority what they think it wants to hear. So perhaps Shannon felt this was the best answer to give. It would have been much easier to claim financial woes than to contradict and offend the values and beliefs of the officers judging him.

Regardless of motivation, Shannon and Kehoe were both sentenced to 156 days of military imprisonment, which was later commuted. But even if Shannon had joined the Allies for moral reasons, it would be wrong to extrapolate noble motives to every young man who deserted to join the British infantry. To do so would oversimplify the rationales that impelled thousands of men to go to war. But this is what has often been done since, and what was certainly done at the time. The moral imperatives that drove men to desert were ignored. The simplistic, but politically expedient, financial excuses were over-emphasised.

This was the response from elements of a military and political culture guided by a blinkered vision of Irish neutrality. Unable to tolerate the challenge of dissent, they could only perceive the actions of deserters negatively and were blinded to the possibility that men could be driven to desert by idealism.

But whilst idealism and morality were politically inexpedient motives to ascribe to deserters, the Defence Ministry did readily acknowledge factors like poor barrack accommodation and dissatisfaction with turf cutting duties. Marriage allowances were another source of discontent; the rates were low and they were not given to all married soldiers.

Marriage allowance was paid to help men financially support their families. In the British forces, the regulations were straightforward: All married men were given the allowance after enlistment. The Irish Army's policy was more byzantine. Anyone joining the Army for permanent service after 1 July 1940 wasn't entitled to marriage allowance until he had served for five years. And anyone who joined the Army for the duration of the Emergency wasn't entitled to marriage allowance at all, unless he joined, and married, before 13 March 1941. The result was that some married men experienced difficulties supporting their families, and it was a source of discontent.

Thinking it would stem the flow of desertions, the government approved increases in marriage allowances. But despite this, desertion remained a problem. By 1943, allowances had been raised a number of times, and another motion in Dáil Éireann put by Deputy Alfred Byrne to increase marriage allowances was defeated. In other words, parliament considered that allowances were now adequate.

So the government, and the Army, sought to identify other reasons why men deserted. Another cause of dissatisfaction amongst Irish soldiers was cutting turf. Turf had long been important in Ireland as a means to heat homes; even some power stations burned turf. Given the growing shortages of raw materials, like oil and coal, as German U-boats waged unrestricted war against merchant shipping, turf became increasingly important as a fuel source. The winter of 1943 was especially harsh, and men worked long hours in tough conditions cutting turf. The

Army Command recognised turf cutting, in its secret annual report, as having the "potential [to cause] serious discontent – something evidenced by a marked increase in desertions".

It made clear economic and logistical sense to employ Irish troops to cut turf. But the young men who answered their country's call to arms expected to defend against invasion, not spend their days knee-deep in bogs. So, as it became increasingly clear that there was no danger to *their* country, perhaps it is not too surprising that some felt that their duty best lay in going abroad to fight the Nazis.

Of course, the factors leading to the high rate of desertions were complex. Despite this, throughout the war, the Irish Army clung to the belief that "the principal cause of desertion from the Defence Forces, to the British Forces, is the higher rates of pay and allowances (including marriage allowance) in the latter Forces".

The Irish Army was keen to know more about how the supposedly halcyon conditions in the British Army were influencing rates of desertion. Unknown to the Irish Army's soldiers, their letters from abroad were being intercepted and passed on to G2 (Army Intelligence) for censorship. G2 was especially interested in letters coming from members of the British Forces. Many of these were from former members of the Irish Army – deserters writing to their friends in their former units.

There is no indication that men were writing to encourage their friends to desert, and G2 didn't see anything to warrant intervention. They did note, though, that letters often referred "… to the apparently 'ideal' (sic) conditions in the British Army." These comments would, no doubt, have come as a surprise to the British soldiers with whom the Irish Army deserters now served. But the comments are also a telling reflection of conditions and morale in the Irish Army, if the tough and austere conditions of the wartime British Army seemed ideal by comparison.

The Irish Army was also worried that pro-British Irish civilians were helping or inducing their soldiers to desert to join the British armed forces. A circular was sent to Command (regional) Intelligence Officers from G2, asking them to report any "reasonably certain" cases of persons approaching Defence Force soldiers with offers of "civilian employment outside the state". This, in other words, referred to industrial employment in Britain. The Intelligence Officers were also asked to be vigilant for private individuals "… aiding or abetting members of the Defence Forces to desert or join other forces outside the state." "Other forces" referred to the armed forces of any country, though its practical implications were limited to Great Britain.

In August 1941, 2nd Division Intelligence Officers discovered a man in Cavan helping soldiers desert to join the British Army by giving them references. The Intelligence Officers reported their suspicions to the civil authorities, and a prosecution, the first of its kind, was launched. The courts decided that the giving of references to serving soldiers constituted a clear case of aiding and abetting in desertion, and sentenced the man to six months imprisonment. After two months, the court took into account the man's good character and lack of previous convictions, and released him on £10 bail.

There is absolutely no evidence to indicate that the man recruiting in Cavan was employed by the British government to try to induce members of the Irish Army to desert. But the British government did place a number of adverts, in both British and Irish newspapers, for the Royal Air Force, aimed at Irish civilians. This instigated a series of protests to the Irish government from those with nationalist leanings. A letter from the Dundalk branch of Fianna Fáil complained about "English Sunday newspapers publishing articles to stimulate British recruiting in this country, whilst at the same time doing their best to demoralise recruiting for the Irish National Army."

A number of advertisements appeared in *The Cork Examiner*, *The Evening Mail* and other newspapers, seeking recruits for the Royal Air Force. Such advertisements read, "Candidates are required in large numbers for training and service in the Royal Air Force ... for the interesting and responsible duties of Navigators of Aircraft. Pay, after a probationary period, is 12/6 per day with free food and accommodation."

More than 12 shillings a day was an attractive prospect at that time. This has been seized on since, in the specious argument claiming that better pay in the British armed forces persuaded men to desert from the Irish Army. But this supposed mercenary rationale fails to compare like with like. Yes, pay, including flying pay (12 shillings and 6 pence per day *for aircrew only*) in the RAF was higher than infantrymen's wages in the Irish Army. But it was a lot higher than British infantrymen's wages, too. That was because it was paid to reward the dangers involved in flying, just as the Irish Army rewarded its own aircrew with higher wages. And if higher wages were all that men wanted, they could find them in British civilian industry without risking death or injury in the RAF.

The newspapers saw the adverts in purely commercial terms and published them without question. *The Cork Examiner* did approach the Department of Defence but was told that, "there was no law under which the publication of such advertisements was prohibited."

Nonetheless, the Irish government asked the British Air Ministry to stop publishing such advertisements in Irish newspapers. The Air Ministry readily agreed, though ads in British newspapers, circulating freely within Eire, still contained them.

Of course, the best source of comment on the rationale for recruitment is the veterans themselves. Whilst writing this book, I had the privilege of interviewing a number of Irishmen with firsthand experience of World War II service with the British and Irish armed forces. Some of them had deserted from the Irish Army, though the majority had not. They all had opinions about why men deserted from the Irish Army. The following is a representative sample. However, given the historic sensitivities still felt in Ireland, it wasn't surprising that some men spoke to me on condition of anonymity. I've been mindful of their views in the few broad, key-point comments presented below.

Looking for adventure was a common theme amongst all the veterans.

"My brother joined, as he told me himself, for a bit of adventure."

"My father was one of the Irish Army deserters. He saw what was happening [in Europe] ... And he also wanted to travel the world and to look for adventure."

Ken McL., from Dublin, served with the Royal Artillery. He hadn't deserted from the Irish Army himself, but many of the men who served with him in the British Army had. "Lots of fellas from the Irish Army enlisted with me," he revealed. "Some of them had fathers who had been in the British Army in World War I ... Life in the Irish Army was boring and [the deserters] wanted to see what was happening. They wanted some adventure ... in fighting units. And stories had filtered through about atrocities–so that motivated them."

Many veterans came from families that had a tradition of service in the British Army. But there were others whose family backgrounds were strongly republican. I asked each one of them if they, or anyone they knew, had joined for money. None of the veterans themselves said that money had influenced their decision to join the Allies, and they all expressed surprise at the question. Yet descendents of deceased veterans commented about the poor work situation in Ireland during World War II, and speculated that their relatives could have "joined for money". Perhaps it's not surprising that families should have bought into the mercenary rationale; this is the view that was traditionally publicised in the media. But that is not how the surviving veterans see it.

Richard Fellows reacted with frank incredulity to the suggestion that he, or anyone else, might have joined for monetary reasons. A sense of adventure and a family tradition of service with the British forces did influence him, though. And he joined the RAF in 1942, as a navigator and bomb aimer, knowing just how dangerous it would be.

"You couldn't listen to the news in 1940 without hearing about the losses," Richard Fellows said. "We knew what we were getting into."

Gerry O'Neill joined the Irish Navy but soon became bored with the inactivity. He was also inspired, to some extent, by the actions of other Irishmen – men like Paddy Finucane, who became a famous fighter ace with the RAF. Gerry was strongly republican by sentiment and wouldn't have been an obvious recruit for service with the British armed forces. "My feelings changed over time as events in Europe unfolded," he said. Money was never a factor in his decision to go to war.

Ken McL. was equally scornful of the idea. "The money was buttons … I got 2 shillings a day as a gunner. Out of this, I paid 6 pence a week for barrack damages and had to buy toiletries and so on. [There was] not much left after all that. In fact, the Salvation Army used to give us envelopes an' paper, so we could write home."

Derek Overend, a Trinity College (Dublin) student and member of the Local Defence Force, certainly didn't join for money. As a university graduate in the 1940s, his employment prospects were excellent. He was far better educated than the majority of men who served with the Irish Army or Local Defence Force. He remembers discussing the prospect of war whilst still at college.

"We all had 3rd level education," he said. "We had meetings about what was best to do for Ireland. The Trinity view was that it was best to stop the Jerrys [Germans] getting England. We wanted to stop them there before they could get to us."

Many other Irishmen shared the belief that fascism was something that had to be confronted. This included men from families with staunch republican leanings. Thomas Walsh remembered the uprising in 1916 and the civil war. As a child, he and his friends would run with messages hidden in their mouths for the IRA and, if stopped by the British Army, would swallow those missives. But in 1939, Walsh joined the British Army. He saw "Europe and democracy threatened by Hitler and German occupation … and so joined up to fight in the British Army against fascism."

Phil Farrington deserted from the Irish Army to serve with the British Army for a more adventurous life. But as the war progressed, he saw what the Nazis had done to Europe, especially in the concentration camps, and his feelings changed. "I cared more about these things near the end [of the war], when I'd seen a few things," he said.

A number of other Irish veterans made similar observations. But perhaps the last word should be left with Paddy Sutton, from Dublin, who served with the RAF. He remembers standing in Bergen-Belsen concentration camp, soon after it was liberated from the SS, and talking about the war with a friend. "My pal turned to me," Paddy recalled. "He said, 'If we ever needed a reason to have joined up, this is it – it was a just war.' I agreed with him. It really hit home then, what an evil regime we'd been fighting."

Few people still alive have the moral authority gained from fighting in World War II, and then standing at the side of the mass graves of the Holocaust whilst they pondered what it was all about. I hope that Paddy Sutton's words, as well as the frank recollections of the other men quoted here, finally lay the money myth to rest.

Chapter 6

Con Murphy: Deserter or Hero?

Cornelius Murphy, Con to his friends, was a farm worker at the outbreak of World War II. His world then was the quiet toil of rural Ireland – early mornings and long days working on the land. Television had yet to insinuate itself into the corner of every room, and the news, for those who wanted it, came from the occasional wireless set and the daily newspaper.

During our interview, I asked Con what he'd thought about Hitler and the Nazis, and whether he and his fellow farm workers had followed events in Europe.

"I knew a bit, but not much," he admitted. "I was working with a farmer and earning about £12 a year – 5 shillings a week. We used to milk the cows by hand and send the milk into the creamery in the morning. Some fellas – farmers or farmers' boys – would be buying a newspaper, so I knew a bit about what was going on, and I thought the Allies were winning. But I didn't know about the concentration camps and things like that."

Early in the war, Con joined the Irish Army and was stationed in West Cork with the 31st Infantry Brigade. He was part of an Emergency battalion. Some experienced soldiers were promoted as NCOs, but the rank and file consisted mainly of new recruits. The battalion spent a considerable amount of time cutting turf to burn as fuel in the power stations.

"I was browned off with the Army and cutting turf – it wasn't soldiering at all," Con told me. "I'd been a farm worker before the war, and I was as badly off in the Irish Army as I'd been then. So I just wanted to get away from it. There was a good few lads disappearing [deserting] in the battalion I was in. You'd hear no more and see no more of them. And I made enquiries about the way to do it."

Con wrote to the RAF and told them he wanted to enlist. He gave his mother's address. Obviously, he didn't want his intentions to become known back at his barracks. And the RAF would never have replied to him there anyway. Then he warned his mother to expect a letter and asked her to hold on to it for him.

"I got impatient waiting for the letter, so I went into Cork intending to go AWOL," Con said. "I stayed in a bed-and-breakfast place for a couple of nights. Whilst I was in Cork, I noticed this fella watching me. I kept bumping into him and I got suspicious. I walked out of the B-and-B in the morning and he was there. I asked him what he was up to."

"He was an innocent young lad really – just a

youngster in the army. It seems that when he joined the army, they asked him did he want to join the Secret Service and he'd said he did. He admitted he was watching me. I guess they'd got suspicious that I was up to something."

The Irish Army did monitor soldiers' movements and secretly intercepted mail. So it's perfectly feasible that this man was working for the Intelligence Services or a branch of the Military Police. Regardless of the man's status, Con made his feelings plain.

"I told him to clear off as fast as he could – or else. Then I went back into my digs. I had a second-hand bike that I'd bought, and I cycled to my home. Then I waited until it was dark and went to the station and got a train to Dublin. I did get stopped by one policeman, but I just told him I'd had my call-up papers. So I stayed overnight in Dublin and, the next day, got on the train to the North."

"There was about 20 men in my carriage," Con continued. "You could tell they were soldiers [deserting]. Anyway, there was no other reason for travelling to the North. There was one fella lived down the road from me. I knew him well to see him, and he knew me, but we didn't say anything. Then a man came on checking tickets and asking everyone if they were in the Irish Army. Of course, we all said no."

Con is unsure about the official's exact status, but thinks the man may have been Customs or the Garda.

"[The official] asked one man if he was in the Irish Army. He said, 'No'. But the official pointed that the man was wearing an army belt. Then the official said, 'When you arrive at the station, you'll be picked up.' What happened to him later, I don't know – I don't know if they sent him back or not. But I know this: The British and Irish governments were working together. And the Irish government was keeping the Germans happy, too, in their own way."

There often seems to be a gap between the official regulations regarding travel documents and the actual experiences veterans recall. So I asked Con if he'd needed a travel document, or pass, to get over the border.

"No, I just had a voucher from the RAF. You were allowed to travel from the South to the North. I think this would have been around the end of 1942 or early 1943. Anyway, when I arrived, someone met us, and I eventually ended up in Newtownards, where I had a medical [exam], which I passed. Then I had to fill out lots of forms with my name and address and so forth. There was a man next to me who couldn't read or write. He was on to me the whole time – 'Would you mind, would you mind …' I did fill in some of it for him, but I had enough to do filling in my own."

Then I asked Con if the RAF had asked him if he was in the Irish Army. His answer was intriguing.

"No, not at *that* stage," he said. "Now, I can't remember it all, but we went to England [for recruit training]. There was lots of square bashing [parade drill]. The English and Irish were all together. We were treated very good compared to the Irish Army."

Conditions in the RAF were better than in the *British*

Army, too. Many wartime servicemen comment on this, and ex-soldiers delight in pointing out that they slept in blankets whilst airmen slept in sheets.

I asked Con if he had ever experienced any discrimination for being Irish.

"No, not at all, there was no question of it. Several times the young fellas who were conscripts would say, 'It isn't your war at all – why are you here?' They couldn't get over that we'd volunteered. I told them we just wanted to see life – something like that."

"In England, during [recruit] training, there was an officer," Con said. "He was watching. He knew we were trained already. Some time afterwards, I was called to see this officer. He said he was going to ask me a few questions. He said, 'If you tell me the truth, there'll be nothing else – no comebacks; you won't be in trouble of any kind'."

"Then he said, 'I'm investigating a few things.' I didn't know what he meant then, though I knew after, all right. He asked me if I was from the Irish Army. I told him I was. Then he asked me what my army number was and unit and so forth. He was smiling to himself as I answered. All he was doing was ticking them off. He [already] had this information in front of him. When we finished, he said 'Good man'.

"I could have been a German spy, of course. At that time, there were rumours that, at night, there were Germans landing [in Ireland] by parachute. And they didn't want them pretending to be Irish, an' then joining up [to carry out sabotage]. This was my own opinion of why I was being questioned. Anyway, I never heard any more about it."

This might sound a little fanciful today. But German agents did parachute into Ireland, though they were usually swiftly caught. And German agents had worked behind the lines as fifth columnists, carrying out acts of sabotage during the invasion of France. In any case, the Irish and British governments were certainly exchanging information about the thousands of Irish Army deserters. And this information was detailed enough to accurately identify individuals. Another indication, perhaps, that after the war when the Irish government court-martialled the dead men, they were well aware of what they were doing.

After his interview with the officer, Con completed his training and volunteered to serve overseas, not knowing where this would take him. Eventually, he found himself on a troopship leaving Liverpool, in a large convoy heading to the Middle East. German U-boats were patrolling the north Atlantic and Mediterranean, attacking and sinking large numbers of ships, though Con was fortunate and his ship reached its destination.

Con spent the next two years working as part of an RAF Embarkation Unit in Haifa. And whilst, in his own words, he was young and carefree, his future in Ireland did sometimes concern him.

"It was in my mind that I'd have to come home and that we'd still be considered deserters. But it was something that was never discussed between me and the other Irish airmen. In fact, I had a pal in Haifa who came from the same town. But I never said to him I'd been in the Irish Army," Con admitted.

"Anyhow, just before D-Day, I was transferred to a camp right out in the desert. One day I wasn't well and I went to see the doctor. I ended up in hospital and was eventually discharged for medical reasons."

I asked Con what he did after the war.

"When the war was finished, Dev [De Valera] pardoned all the deserters from the Irish Army who joined the Allies. I knew, because I was sent a cutting from the paper from back home. That left me free to come back."

Con feels (rightly) that this was not an act of kindness, approval, or gratitude on behalf of the State: "They just didn't have enough jails to put us all into," Con said.

Con struggled to find work in Ireland. Of course, it was a difficult time for everyone. But an added problem for Con was having his name on the List, which prevented him from even being considered for most jobs. He knew about the List because his brother, a sergeant in the Irish Army, saw a copy of it in the town hall.

"But I had a small pension from the RAF for medical reasons, and they didn't discharge me officially till 1948," Con explained. "So I was still getting paid. I was very happy with the way I was getting treated [by the RAF]. They looked after me – no doubt about it."

Aside from the issue of the List, I asked Con how his friends and neighbours in Ireland had treated him when he returned.

"People were just looking for something to eat," he said. "They didn't care about anything else. And the [Irish] army never had a good name around here, anyway."

Con went to England to find work but eventually returned to Ireland. He married and had children. He still receives his pension from the RAF.

Chapter 7

Travel Permits: An Unhappy State of Affairs

The Holyhead and Dún Laoghaire ferry, between Eire and Britain, continued running throughout the war. One Irishman serving in the RAF describes going home on leave as a straightforward arrangement.

"I was given a suit of civvy clothes at Chelsea Barracks to travel home in," Paddy Sutton told me. "I got the ferry from Holyhead to Dún Laoghaire. There was a special gangway for British servicemen. The British MPs [military police] stayed on the boat. They kept out of sight when the boat arrived in Dún Laoghaire. I just got off the boat, no one checked my pass, and I didn't notice anyone especially watching who arrived."

This happy state of affairs didn't last very long. Passengers landing at Dún Laoghaire had to fill in a landing card with personal details prior to entering Ireland. Irish members of the British armed forces, returning to Ireland on leave, were instructed by the British authorities not to give the full details and address of their military unit. They merely wrote "c/o War Office, Admiralty or Air Ministry, London", as appropriate. This was simply a wartime confidentiality measure, aimed at preventing German intelligence-gathering within Ireland. Britain and the USA were especially sensitive about this, given the Irish government's refusal to close down the German Legation in Dublin.

The landing card system initially worked well. But in early 1942, servicemen returning to Ireland on leave were pressured to divulge details of their military unit's location. In some cases, men were told they would be denied entry to the country unless they did. This was a dreadful threat to a young soldier going on leave to see his family. For many of these men facing imminent combat and death, it could well be a final visit.

So the British government complained to the Irish government, and a compromise was readily made. Colonel Dan Bryan, now head of G2 in Dublin, saw the British position as a "reasonable military precaution, which we would ourselves take in similar circumstances". He agreed that soldiers would not be asked to state their exact address in England. In return, the British authorities agreed to have all service cards specially stamped at Holyhead.

Like many wartime arrangements between Ireland and the UK, this one was negotiated, and implemented, discreetly and semi-officially. Bryan wrote a letter, marked "personal and secret," to Fred Boland at the Department of External Affairs. Bryan wanted the instruction to the Department of Justice that would implement the agreement to appear to be from External Affairs: "My status in the matter would not be apparent to them [in Justice]," he said.

Obligingly, External Affairs requested that the Department of Justice instruct immigration officials to desist from asking for specific addresses. Immigration denied having done so in the first place and suggested that it was the civilian police. The civilian police, in turn, revealed that it was actually the Military Police that were questioning members of the British forces whom they suspected to be deserters from the Irish Army.

It was the Military Police's duty to capture deserters, so their actions aren't surprising. Then, having been hindered in their attempts at the ferry port, they redoubled their efforts on the border with Northern Ireland. The Provost Marshal, or senior military policeman, instituted a system of reporting absentees to Garda stations and the Detective Division in Dublin Castle. Being forewarned, this enabled the Garda, in conjunction with the Military Police, to catch many of the deserters on trains and at border crossing points en route to Northern Ireland.

So, during 1942, the authorities recaptured 72 percent of the men who deserted. Of course, word of the new measures soon spread amongst the troops, and the number recaptured during 1943 fell to 34 percent. According to G2, "… in so far as deserters are joining the British Forces, the normal routes and procedure of entry into Northern Ireland is being avoided."

In other words, many deserters were avoiding

checkpoints by crossing the border on foot, using the maze of country lanes and paths that crisscrossed between the North and the South. The authorities stepped up patrols along the border to stem the flow of deserters crossing, but it was virtually impossible to police effectively. The porous border did sometimes lead to amusing incidents, though: A soldier, in the Royal Ulster Rifles, was out on a training route march in Northern Ireland one day.

"The young English officer leading us noticed some of the platoon complaining to each other. During a water break, seeing that some of the men were visibly upset, he asked the platoon sergeant to see what was up with them. A few minutes later the sergeant reported back. He told the officer that we'd been in the Free State [Republic] for the last four miles and the soldiers who were deserters from the Irish Army were getting a bit worried..."[5]

Of course, [Southern] Irish polity saw Ireland as one country without internal boundaries. This left them with a dilemma. In practice, the Irish government needed to monitor and police the border to catch Irish Army deserters. But in principle, they aspired to a borderless Ireland with free passage to the North. Meanwhile, the situation was viewed very differently from a Northern Ireland perspective, as its government failed to share the united Irish aspirations of Dublin. And, as part of the United Kingdom, Northern Ireland felt themselves very much a government and people at war.

5 Writer prefers to remain anonymous

Border controls were imposed on the northern side of the border in July 1940. The Northern Ireland government passed legislation requiring anyone in Northern Ireland, aged 14 and over, to hold an approved identity document. For Southern Irish citizens visiting the North, this could be a national registration identity card, a passport, a travel permit, or an identity document issued by the Royal Ulster Constabulary.

Eire had already taken one step toward dealing with border issues. In September 1939, a system of travel permits had been implemented for anyone wanting to travel abroad. This legislation applied to travellers destined for any county, although, for most people, it meant Great Britain. Applying for a permit was straightforward: Applicants had to hand in a completed application form to their nearest Garda station; Dublin residents had to apply to the Garda Passport Office in Palace Street.

The Garda were responsible for applying Department of Justice guidelines to decide whether the applicant was "a fit and proper person to receive a passport or travel permit". They then certified the form and passed it on to the Ministry of External Affairs. The Department also operated its own "Stop List" of certain named individuals, though it generally relied on the Garda's enquiries to establish *bona fides*.

In 1941, Michael Baggott, a shop assistant from Abbeyleix, applied for a travel permit to travel to Liverpool, England. He signed the application form, enclosed his birth certificate, and added two countersigned photographs of himself. Then he sent in his application, unaware that he was about to cause a minor furore within the Irish government.

Baggott stated that the purpose of his journey was "to join the British Army". This degree of candour was his first mistake. The government responded with a memo to the Department of Justice, regarding anyone applying for travel permits to join the [British] fighting forces: "It is undesirable that this should appear on our forms … what should normally be stated … is *business*."

In other words, issuing travel permits to join the British Army was officially acceptable. But it should be done discreetly. Mr. Baggot erred further, though. He provided a full length photograph, instead of the officially sanctioned head and shoulder view. But the real blunder was using a photograph dressed in his uniform as a serving member of the Local Defence Force (LDF). These photographs were signed by a Garda sergeant and countersigned by a Garda superintendant. This was normal procedure, but not in the case of a serving member of the LDF.

In a mild admonishment, the Department of Justice arranged for "appropriate instructions to be sent to the Guards in this matter". And Mr. Baggot was simply requested to re-submit "two passport photographs … in *civilian* attire". The Department of External Affairs then queried whether Baggott needed the permission of the Military Authorities to leave the country during wartime. This, like many other contentious issues, was referred on to Major Dan Bryan in G.2 Branch.

It isn't clear just how widespread the practice of issuing travel permits to regular and reserve soldiers was. And it's even less clear to what extent, if at all, police officers colluded in helping soldiers desert. But the seeming ease with which travel permits were issued reveals something about attitudes toward the war amongst some sectors of the populace.

Derek Overend also left the Local Defence Force, and joined the British Army in early 1941. He recalls, "The LDF were helpful when I wanted to leave."

Overend joined the Royal Artillery as an officer and served in the D-Day landings, and was attached to the 101st Airborne Division at Arnhem. He'd been less than thrilled with service in the LDF, "running around [Dundrum] without weapons, looking for paratroopers." And he'd had no difficulty getting a travel permit to leave.

Naturally, with high levels of unemployment, an ailing economy, and the benefit of sterling remittances from thousands of workers in the UK, the government had no incentive to make the issue of travel permits more cumbersome than necessary. But the matter was brought to a head again when Private Griffen, 8th Thomond Battalion, was caught leaving the country in November 1941. He was apprehended by the Military Police, in possession of a travel permit, boarding the mail boat at Dún Laoghaire. Griffen was on "indefinite leave" at the time. Nonetheless, as a serving soldier, he wasn't allowed to leave the country without permission, and the Ministry of Defence (MOD) considered him to be an intending deserter.

The MOD consulted with the Ministry of External Affairs and the Department of Justice "to prevent the use of permits as an aid to desertion from the Defence Forces". The first measure was to place the onus on the Garda to screen permit applications for members of the Defence Forces. Given that applications had to be made at the Garda Station nearest to the applicant's home, this made sense, especially in smaller towns and rural areas, where the local Garda would be more in tune with the activities of the populace.

The second proposal was to put an additional question on the application; form TP1(a). Question 16 already asked for the applicant's occupation. The additional question, to be inserted after this, would ask the applicant specifically if he was, or had ever been, a member of the Defence Forces. Correspondence about this dragged on between the various government departments. Pragmatic considerations held things up further, as large quantities of form TP1(a) were still held in stock and wastage was not encouraged.

Meanwhile, desertions from the Irish Army continued. Some men made it across the border to join the Allies. Some were apprehended by the Military Police. And the MOD continued to grumble over the issue of travel permits. The matter resurfaced yet again in 1942 when John Bird, a reservist from Dublin, was caught by the Military Police en route to Scotland.

Members of the Defence Forces were allowed to leave the country for up to 28 days. Bird had applied for and received a travel permit via the Garda. But he hadn't requested permission from his commanding officer. And he'd neglected to mention his military status on form TP1(a). Yet again, the MOD raised the issue of having a specific question added to the form. They were told by the Department of External Affairs that the issue was "under consideration." Matters dragged on for the rest of the year, with inter-departmental bickering over the wording of the question. External Affairs also seemed keen not to inconvenience men who had retired from the Defence Forces as long ago as 1923, who might not readily be able to furnish proof of discharge to the Garda.

Agreement was eventually reached in March 1943, and the wording of the question was changed to: "Have you at any time been, or are you at present, a member of the Defence Forces of Ireland? If so, [a] certificate of discharge or military pass authorising your proposed period of absence … must be attached."

However, preventing desertions wasn't as simple as altering the wording on a government form: Thousands of men continued to cross the border without travel permits. And Baggot, Griffen, and Bird were just three men, whose cases highlighted a situation and served as a catalyst for government action. Perhaps it's invidious to single them out again now to illustrate another point. Aside from the issue of travel permits, those men have one other thing in common: They were *caught* in the act of deserting, and their names were not added to the List.

Of course, many men with travel permits were not

caught. For instance, Cornelius Kelly, from Dublin, was serving with the 2nd Medium (Anti-Aircraft) Battery at McKee Barracks. In 1940, he applied for a travel permit to visit Belfast. As he had his Commanding Officer's permission, it was granted. Later, in 1942, he used the permit to travel to Northern Ireland and desert from the army. He wasn't caught, and his name eventually went on the List, whilst deserters who *were* caught avoided that fate. So the matter of travel permits also highlights the discriminatory effect, and almost arbitrary nature, of the List.

Chapter 8

Gerry O'Neill and the Empress of Asia

In August 2009, I spoke with Gerry O'Neill. Gerry was born in Fermoy and grew up in North Dublin. He joined the newly formed Irish Navy in 1940, as an engineering rating. Speaking in a clear, educated, articulate manner that belied his 91 years, he told me a little about his amazing wartime career. He was also curious about my own background and, when I told him I was from Liverpool, he ribbed me about my accent. He laughed whilst we reminisced about long demolished areas of Liverpool, such as Scotland Road, familiar to generations of Irish migrants.

Clearly a man with a great sense of humour, he recalled one incident during his service with the Irish Navy during World War II, or the Emergency, as it was then called in Ireland.

Not long before Gerry left the Navy, the Irish Army carried out some manoeuvres. The Army's task was to guard the coast against seaborne invasion, and Army HQ decided to test some of the units involved. Gerry was in charge of a group of naval ratings given the task of attacking a detachment of soldiers guarding an old Martello Tower on the coast.

Gerry recounted with relish how his men, armed with old Lee Enfield rifles and bayonets, advanced along the side of a cornfield to the tower.

"I looked over the side of a ditch, whilst my men stayed undercover. There were about 20 [Irish] soldiers with not a rifle to be seen. Seven or eight men were sat at a table drinking bottles of stout [ale] and playing cards. The rest were asleep in the grass or sunbathing. And they certainly weren't watching for an invasion from the sea," he said.

"I told my men to fix bayonets, and we charged at the soldiers. Then I shouted [in Irish], '*Seassus agus cuir suas do láimh*', which means 'Stand up and put up your hands'. I doubt if anyone understood this," Gerry said. "One of the card players knocked over the table and screamed, 'Jaysus, it's the fuckin' Germans.' Another soldier, who must have watched too many war films, waved a white handkerchief and kept saying '*kamerade, kamerade*'. And one poor man knelt down in front of us and said, 'Don't shoot me – I'm a married man with five children'."

So the exercise was a success for the Irish Navy. They made 'prisoners' of the Irish soldiers who clearly hadn't seen an Irish Navy uniform before and thought they were from the German Navy.

But there would soon be another group of soldiers,

with far more cause to be grateful to the Irish Navy. The Irish government had bought some Motor Torpedo Boats (MTB) from a British shipyard. This was just before the Dunkirk evacuation, between May 26 and June 4, 1940. Following the German *blitzkrieg*, the British – and elements of the French Army that hadn't surrendered to the Germans – had retreated to Dunkirk. The Royal Navy, aided by an armada of civilian boats and ships of every description, was evacuating the British Army from the beaches, under a relentless German artillery and aerial bombardment. Further inland, the beachhead was being protected by British and French troops, who mounted a savage rearguard action and delayed the Germans long enough for most of the Army to be evacuated.

Meanwhile, Gerry was in England as part of the crew bringing MTB2 back to Ireland.

"We were in Southampton, taking over the MTB from Thornycroft," Gerry recalled. "Our skipper had been in the Royal Navy, and he decided to join the rescue fleet. He asked us if we'd volunteer, which we did. We made two trips across the channel. The idea was to get in [to the beach] and get out – fast."

I asked Gerry what the beaches at Dunkirk had looked like during the evacuation.

"There were thousands of men on the beaches," he replied. "You know, Churchill had given orders [to the Royal Navy] to leave the wounded men till last. They needed to bring back as many able-bodied men as possible, to defend Britain against invasion. But we brought back mostly walking wounded. Those lads didn't know who we were. I think they thought we were Free French [Forces], because we had FF on our caps."

Then I asked Gerry if his MTB had been fired on by the Germans.

"No," he said. "The *Luftwaffe* went for bigger ships, like the [Royal Navy] destroyers."

"But would you [the Irish Navy] have fired on the Germans if they had attacked you?" I asked.

"Oh, yes," he answered. Then he said, with what sounded like regret, "We didn't need to fire [at the German bombers], but we'd have loved to."

MTB2 made two trips over to Dunkirk, returning laden with wounded British soldiers. The potential repercussions for neutral Ireland, if an Irish Navy vessel had fired on German aircraft or been sunk off the French coast whilst helping to evacuate the British troops, were serious. And after the second trip, the crew were advised by the British authorities not to go again. But it had been a gallant and generous act, rescuing wounded soldiers in their hour of need.

When MTB2 returned to the naval base at Haulbowline, in Cork, the crew were sworn to secrecy about their Dunkirk escapade.

"After this, I soon got browned off with the inactivity in the Irish Navy – and I decided to join the RAF," Gerry said.

So he cycled from Cork to Dublin, where he met up with a friend. They cycled up to Newry in Northern

Ireland, sold their bicycles, and took the train to Belfast. They were provisionally accepted for aircrew training, but were told they'd have to wait a few weeks to receive call-up papers. So they headed back to Newry and bought their bikes back. Then Gerry cycled back to Cork to re-join his MTB, with the Irish Navy no wiser about his intention to desert.

Gerry had asked the RAF to send his call-up papers to his parents' address. When the papers arrived, his parents tore them up and didn't tell him. Unaware of this, he grew tired of waiting and went to Belfast and joined the British Merchant Navy as an engineer. He was sent to Liverpool, where he signed on as an engineer on the Empress of Asia. He used a false name: Harry Robertson.

A few months later, the Empress called into Bombay, where troops were picked up en route to Singapore. There were other Irish deserters amongst the soldiers, though Gerry was unaware of this at the time. One of them was Patrick Moran, of the 18th Reconnaissance Battalion, whose story is told in the next chapter.

The Empress was attacked by Japanese bombers a few miles from Singapore and was abandoned after being hit.

"Some of the stokers were trapped down below and the ship was on fire," Gerry remembered. "I was on the stern and got onboard the [Australian warship] Yarra, which was taking men off the ship. The Yarra took us into Singapore. We stayed in a schoolhouse for a while. Then we went into Raffles [hotel] for a few days. A young RN Lieutenant came in looking for engineers. So I was sent to join a small ship, called the Ampang, whose native crew had abandoned her."

The new crew's task was to help evacuate women and children, and take them to Java before the Japanese overran Singapore. Lacking enough fuel to make it to Java, the crew sailed to Palambang, Sumatra. They came under attack from Japanese bombers whilst entering harbour and made a hurried escape just in front of the Japanese troops, who landed less than an hour later. Gerry, along with some friends, went overland to Oesthaven in southern Sumatra. Still keeping one step ahead of the Japanese, they got on the last ship to leave. They sailed to Sumatra and eventually escaped on an Australian ship before the Japanese invaded.

After returning to the UK in 1942, Gerry decided to pay a visit to his family in Ireland; luckily, he wasn't spotted and arrested when entering the country. He went to Dublin, where he bumped into an old friend who was involved in the formation of Irish Shipping Ltd. This was a new merchant shipping company, which was looking for engineers for some ships it had just bought. So, seizing the opportunity, Gerry signed on an ageing steamship, renamed the Irish Larch.

But Gerry was still, officially, a deserter from the Irish Navy. He solved this with what he described as "an Irish solution to an Irish problem."

"The General Manager of Irish Shipping hosted a reception onboard the Irish Larch for the Irish Cabinet, including the Taoiseach [Eamon De Valera]," Gerry said.

"Later in the evening, the Cabinet gave a dinner for the ship's officers in the Hotel Commodore, Cobh. After the wine had flowed freely, I took the opportunity to make my 'confession' to Oscar Traynor, the Minister of Defence. I told him I'd deserted from the Irish Navy and asked if I could be pardoned, in view of the fact that I was now a greater help to the nation, serving with Irish Shipping, exposed to all sorts of dangers crossing the sub[marine] infested North Atlantic."

"He asked me to leave the matter with him," Gerry continued. "A few days later, I received an official communication confirming my release [from the Irish Navy] because of the difficulty in finding suitable crews for the vessels being acquired [for the merchant service]."

After serving a little longer with the Irish Larch, Gerry returned to the UK and went to sea again with the British Merchant Navy. He served on the hazardous Arctic convoys, taking supplies out to the Soviet Union. These convoys of merchant ships, and their warship escorts, suffered nearly 50 percent losses on some of the voyages. German U-boats sunk many of them, and the survivors stood little chance of survival in the icy arctic seas where men froze to death in minutes. Eventually, Gerry transferred to the Royal Canadian Navy and served on a corvette escorting the North Atlantic convoys.

Later in the war, his ship was transferred to duties in the Pacific theatre. They patrolled the seas off the island of Iwo Jima, hunting for Japanese submarines, whilst the US Marine Corps were in the final stages of the battle for the island. After this, the corvette took part in the great naval battle of Okinawa. Again, its role was to detect and destroy Japanese submarines. But the subs never materialised. This left the corvette in a prime position to watch the destruction of the Japanese battleship Yamato – the biggest battleship in the world. That was where Gerry's war finished.

He was in the engine room, taking temperature readings, when a shell burst through the hull of the ship and hit the condenser. A jet of steam and boiling water hit the front of his body. "I can't remember feeling any pain – I must have passed out immediately," he said. "When I came to, I found myself on deck, amongst corpses and wounded Japanese that we'd picked up."

Gerry was transported to an American hospital ship and then to a US Navy hospital in Pearl Harbour. When his wounds were healed, he was sent to Canada and discharged from the Royal Canadian Navy. After the war, Gerry returned to Ireland and enjoyed a long and successful career, initially at sea, with the Shell and B.P. oil companies.

Sadly, a few weeks after giving this interview, Gerry O'Neill passed away.

PART II

Chapter 9

Far East: Descent into Hell

On 8 December 1941[6], the Japanese made their infamous surprise attack on the American Pacific Fleet at Pearl Harbour. On the same day, they also attacked the British in Hong Kong and Malaya. The Japanese army landed in northern Malaya and Thailand. Then they swept down through the Malayan peninsula, opposed by British, Australian, and local Malay forces, in a series of bloody and desperate rearguard actions, until the fall of Singapore in February 1942.

Irish Army deserter Patrick Moran was serving in India as a private in the newly formed 18th Battalion, Reconnaissance Regiment. The battalion was in Bombay when it received orders to proceed to Singapore.

The battalion embarked on the Empress of Asia, which sailed for Singapore on 23 January 1942, carrying over 2,200 soldiers. Moran stood on deck, with the rest of the 18th Reconnaissance Battalion, watching the coast recede

6 Japanese time

as the ship left the safety of Bombay. The Empress of Asia had been rescued from the scrap yard in 1939, and she was dirty and old. It wasn't going to be the most comfortable voyage. Nonetheless, most of the men were eager to get into action and wave India goodbye.

A little under three weeks later, the Empress of Asia, in convoy with some other vessels, arrived at the Banka Straights approaching Singapore. HMS Exeter, the cruiser made famous at the battle of the River Plate against the German battleship Graf Von Spee, led the convoy in line astern through the straights. A formation of 18 Japanese aeroplanes flew overhead at high altitude. One of them dropped a stick of bombs, which landed perilously close to the Empress. Columns of water erupted into the air, and shell splinters flew across the decks. But no one was injured and the convoy sailed onwards.

Later that morning, the faster ships left the convoy. The three remaining ships, including the Empress, headed toward Singapore accompanied by HMS Danae. After steaming through the night, they arrived at the Sultan Shoal, on the approaches to Singapore, on 5 February 1942. It was a clear, pleasant, sunny day with good visibility – ideal weather for the Japanese bombers that attacked the convoy in waves at 11:00 that morning.

Coming in from all directions, the Japanese bombers dived down to around 3,000 feet, releasing their bombs. In return, the troopships and the naval escorts opened fire on the aircraft. The scene was a maelstrom of exploding bombs, erupting waterspouts, and the noise of anti-aircraft guns. A few minutes after the attack started, a bomb hit the Empress on the starboard side near the funnel; about 10 minutes later, two or three more bombs hit the ship.

Most of the troops were sheltering below deck, but about 20 minutes after the attack started, it became clear that the ship would have to be abandoned. Captain Smith gave orders for the troops to go to their muster stations on A Deck. By now, the exploding bombs had started fires down below, and the engine room was abandoned.

At 12:00, the Japanese planes broke off the attack. The Empress was about 10 or 11 miles off Singapore, and Captain Smith ordered the forecastle crew to drop the anchors. Thick black smoke, and the heat and flames from the fires, effectively divided the ship in two as the midship part of the vessel burned. An Australian sloop, HMAS Yarra, came alongside the Empress's stern. Many of the soldiers mustered there were able to step directly across, and the Yarra rescued around 1,000 men, (including Gerry O'Neill[7]).

The situation on the Empress's forecastle was more precarious. The troops climbed down ropes into the sea, where small boats waited to pick up the survivors. Many men were transferred by boat, temporarily, to the nearby Sultan Shoal Lighthouse, and some men managed to swim there. Trooper Moran struggled in the water, until finally being picked up by a boat. A few men drowned, and sharks killed at least one soldier. But, eventually, the troops were landed at Singapore Docks and taken to billets at Geyland Road.

7 See previous chapter

A convoy of trucks took the wounded men to the 1st Malayan General Hospital, a military field hospital set up at Selarang army barracks. The 18th Reconnaissance Battalion set up their HQ at Choon Guan School. The battalion's weapons and equipment were onboard the Empress of Asia, which was sinking, and surplus equipment was in short supply. So initially, the men were just given groundsheets, blankets, and mosquito nets. The next day, they were issued with some rifles and Bren guns.

Whilst the battalion was being re-equipped, Patrick Moran, who was feeling ill, reported to the battalion medical officer and was sent to the hospital at Selarang. According to a witness statement from Lieutenant Hargreaves, a Reconnaissance Battalion officer, this was on either 6 or 7 February.

On 11 February, four days before Singapore surrendered to the Japanese, the patients from the field hospital at Selarang barracks were evacuated to Alexandra Hospital. The hospital had been built in 1940, in the colonial style, with long shaded verandahs and tranquil, well-tended lawns and gardens – though it didn't look quite like this by the time the patients from Selarang Barracks arrived there.

Moran, a medical patient, was taken to the hospital reception before being allocated to a ward. Corporal Pease, another of the wounded from the Empress of Asia, described the sight that met new arrivals at reception.

"… what chaos, wounded men, blood, piles of discarded clothing and equipment, all stained with blood and soil, and the smell was terrible. And as fast as [each] ambulance drove up and discharged its load, another was waiting to do the same thing. Nobody can imagine unless they have seen it what a ghastly, horrible, filthy thing it is … men with legs torn off, heads split, [and] intestines ripped out. I cannot put into words, the sights and sounds, the screams of agony."

During the next couple of days, the hospital suffered constant bombardments and air raids as the Japanese Army advanced closer and closer. By Saturday, 14 February, the hospital was positioned in a small enclave between the British and Japanese front lines. During the afternoon, Japanese infantrymen entered the undefended military hospital. The Japanese soldiers ran amok. They shot doctors and medical staff, raped some auxiliary nurses, and bayoneted to death hundreds of unarmed sick and wounded soldiers.

When a British army doctor tried to surrender the hospital to the Japanese in order to protect the patients, a Japanese soldier bayoneted him to death through the white flag he was holding. In the hospital reception area, a Japanese soldier walked around beating wounded Allied soldiers with a broom handle as they lay in their beds. Whilst he was doing this, another Japanese soldier urinated on a dying man who was lying on the floor. The Japanese even bayoneted an anaesthetised patient on an operating table.

In another part of the building, Dr. Allardyce, a former student from Trinity College, Dublin, was being held under guard with some other medical staff. Just before nightfall, the Japanese asked for a doctor. Then they took him away, along with two Royal Army Medical Corps stretcher-bearers. The following day Dr. Allardyce was found outside, bayoneted to death. One of the stretcher-bearers was also bayoneted, and the other was found dead with shrapnel wounds.

More Japanese soldiers went into the medical wards where Trooper Moran was. They bayoneted many of the staff and patients. The ones who were capable of walking were taken into the main corridor. Then they were dragged outside, where around 200 British, Indian, Australian, and Malayan patients and staff were gathered together. These men, many of whom were already badly wounded, were beaten and then tied up. Those who couldn't manage to stand were killed. The survivors, including Moran, unless he had already been murdered, were taken to some buildings on the other side of the Ayer Rajah Road.

At least 200 prisoners were crammed into three rooms. Each unventilated room measured approximately 10 feet by 10 feet. The men were crushed so closely together that they were forced to urinate over each other. During the night, a number of prisoners died of heat stroke and dehydration.

The next day, 15 February, the prisoners were told they were being taken for a drink of water and led from the rooms in pairs. At first, the men left inside the building believed the Japanese soldiers. But "screams of anguish were heard, together with cries in English of 'Oh my God', 'Mother', 'Don't, don't', and groans. Then they saw one of the returning Japanese, wiping blood off his bayonet with a large piece of cloth."[8]

At least 100 men were bayoneted to death before the Japanese were interrupted by artillery fire, which forced them to take cover. One shell blew a hole in the rear of the building and some of the men inside made a run for it. Most of them were machine-gunned by nearby Japanese infantry. But a few prisoners did escape, some of whom survived to bear witness to the massacre.

Patrick Moran was not one of those survivors. He'd been admitted to the hospital a week earlier with what a witness remembered as pneumonia. This was before the advent of antibiotics, and respiratory infections were more often fatal. So it is possible that he, coincidentally, died of pneumonia on 15 February. However, it's much more likely that Trooper Moran died, in agony, on the end of a Japanese bayonet. Three and a half years later, Patrick Moran was court-martialled, *in absentia*, by the Irish government.

★ ★ ★

Gunner Stephen McManus was another Irish Army deserter who had chosen to join the Allies. But, unlike Moran, he survived the final days of fighting before

8 Massacre at the (Alexandra Road) British Military Hospital: eyewitness accounts. Imperial War Museum

Singapore capitulated. He'd arrived in Singapore with 144 Battery (35 Light Anti-Aircraft Regiment), otherwise known as the 35th. The regiment had originally been formed for the air defence of RAF airfields in the UK. Its soldiers tended to be older than average, some of them in their late 40s.

In November 1940, the 35th had left the UK for the Middle East. But, whilst still at sea, the ship was diverted to Singapore and arrived at Keppel docks on 13 January 1941. As the ships came into harbour, 80 Japanese bombers, with their fighter escorts, flew overhead. Torrential rain lashed down, and thick clouds and poor visibility prevented the Japanese from aiming at the convoy. The Japanese dropped their bombs nonetheless. Some bombs fell harmlessly into the sea, missing the ships, much to the relief of the troops onboard. But many exploded in the city, causing more than 200 civilian casualties.

McManus's ship tied up alongside the jetty in Keppel Harbour. The soldiers hurriedly disembarked. After 11 weeks at sea, they were glad to be on dry land again. But their guns, which were on a different ship, had gone on to the Middle East. So they were re-equipped, probably with 40mm Bofors guns, and sent into action. Most of the 35th's two other batteries were sent to Sumatra, but McManus, with 144 Battery, was sent across the causeway into Johore.

The battery shot down a number of Japanese Zero fighters before withdrawing to Singapore a week later when the causeway was blown. Along with the rest of the British and Commonwealth forces, the battery surrendered on 15 February. Two days later, after the victorious Japanese Army entered Singapore, over 52,000 British and Australian soldiers were disarmed and imprisoned in the army barracks at Changi.

The barracks were grossly overcrowded, and the water supplies had been destroyed. The soldiers' first task was to dig wells and try to improvise some sort of sewage system. Initially, the Japanese left them alone, warning them not to attempt escape and threatening execution if they tried. A few soldiers did try, but they were caught and then murdered in a series of brutal executions staged on the beach in front of their despairing comrades.

Conditions in the barracks gradually deteriorated, and food supplies ran low. The Japanese issued the Commonwealth troops with little more than poor quality rice, the sweepings from factory floors, and pieces of rotten fish heaving with maggots. Many men suffered from dysentery, and vitamin deficiency diseases like beriberi became commonplace.

The men sent into Singapore city on working parties had the opportunity to buy food by trading with sympathetic Chinese civilians, using the few personal possessions not already stolen by the Japanese. But the Japanese inflicted severe penalties on any soldiers they caught buying food, and some men were tortured or beaten to death. The soldiers suffered starvation, disease, and bestial treatment at Changi, and worse was yet to come.

The Japanese decided to build a railway linking the existing rail network in Siam to Burma. The railway was built virtually by hand, using slave labour to hack through dense jungle and mountain ranges. Over 18,000 Commonwealth, Dutch, and American prisoners of war, plus 100,000 conscripted Thai, Burmese, and Malay civilians died from starvation, disease, and brutal treatment in the process.

On 17 August, McManus was sent with a party of men to Thailand to work on the Burma Railway. Many of his friends in 144 Battery were kept behind at Changi. Some men were glad to stay behind, on the "better the devil you know" principle. Others, believing the Japanese lies about being sent to new camps where there would be adequate food, good accommodation, and proper medical facilities, were disappointed not to go. And those left behind were right to be disappointed, because their fate was grim indeed.

In October, 600 of these remaining Royal Artillery soldiers, including 126 officers and men from 144 Battery, were put on a ship in Singapore docks. Conditions on the ship were horrendous. Crammed below in the hold, without food, water, ventilation or even any sanitary arrangements, many men died from heat exhaustion, dehydration, and dysentery.

Instead of being taken to Japan, as they were originally told, the men were landed in the Solomon Islands. Eighty-two men, who were so badly sick that they just couldn't work, were left on Rabaul. The remainder were taken to Ballale, to build airfields for the Japanese. The work was all done by hand, without adequate food, water, or any medical care, in baking tropical heat. Starvation and disease took a lethal daily toll, and the Japanese massacred the rest of the men when the job was completed. Out of the original 600 men selected from the Royal Artillery at Changi, only 18 survived the war.

Meanwhile, in Burma, McManus worked in a series of camps along the Burma Railway, where brutality, slave labour, and starvation were the norm. There was little that the soldiers working on the railway could do to make life any better. Anyone with any personal possessions left would exchange them with local traders, for eggs or sometimes a piece of meat. But just as important as food was the will to survive.

The Japanese readily tortured and executed prisoners for the most trivial offences. But, as a morale boost, men still tried to find ways to defy their Japanese guards. Each soldier had a record card, which the Japanese camp authorities kept, with his army details and civilian occupation. When the Japanese wanted skilled tradesmen, such as engineers or electricians, they could check against the records. So, some men put down spurious civilian occupations as a tiny act of defiance that couldn't be immediately detected.

For example, McManus had been a labourer in Sligo. But he convinced the Japanese that he was a professional footballer. It was these little things – the jokes in the face of adversity – that lifted spirits and helped men to struggle on in conditions so grim that sometimes death felt the better option.

As the months progressed, many prisoners died of

malnutrition. The rest were reduced to little more than living skeletons. Christmas 1942 brought a day of respite for most of the camps along the railway, as the Japanese issued a little extra food and allowed the men to have a day off. It was McManus's first Christmas in captivity, and an especially poignant day, as it was also his birthday.

The festivity was one just one day off, in an otherwise unending nightmare of slavery and brutality. And conditions worsened even further, in February 1943, when the Japanese decided they wanted to advance the completion date of the railway. This was the start of what the Japanese called Speedo.

Patrick T, a surviving Irish prisoner of war, recalled some of his experiences for me.

"The Nips [Japanese] were given orders that they had to get the railway finished early," Patrick said. "That summer [July – October 1943] they worked us like slaves. Well, we were slaves really. We worked day an' night with hardly any food, [and] men were dying like flies. My pal collapsed in the heat one day. The guard started hitting him with a bamboo stick. He couldn't get up and the Nip just beat him to death and kicked his body down into the ditch. There was nothing you could do – if you tried to stop them, they would go crazy and you'd get the same. I don't like to think of it really, but I can still see it now."[9]

Patrick faltered and then took a deep breath, clearly struggling with his memories. Then he continued, "I got

9 Interview with an Irish survivor of the POW camps: Given on strict conditions of anonymity.

dysentery lots of times. We'd burn some wood an' make charcoal and eat it – it helped a little. If you got really bad, you'd go to the hospital. Our doctors and medical orderlies did their best to treat the sick, but they didn't have medicines or equipment. I had ulcers on my leg one time, from some tropical disease. I thought I'd go an' ask the Nips for some medicine – I knew they had supplies. It was a stupid thing to do. I should have known better. One of them knocked me to the ground and held me down, whilst this other Jap bastard cut the ulcers off my leg with his feckin bayonet …"

Medical supplies were withheld, and the soldiers' starvation rations didn't change. The Japanese didn't care how many men died from dysentery during the Speedo. And die they did, in the thousands, from dysentery and other preventable diseases like beriberi, diphtheria, and pellagra.

But perhaps one of the most feared diseases, which wiped out men already weakened by malnutrition and overwork, was cholera. Cholera epidemics swept up and down the railway, taking a grim toll on the prisoners. The British and Australian medical orderlies and doctors did their best. But lacking any medicine or proper medical facilities, there was an 80 percent death rate from cholera. The symptoms started with violent diarrhoea, followed by vomiting and abdominal cramps. Most men died within a day or two of catching the disease.

I asked Patrick about the cholera huts – though it was the last question I asked him, as talking about it all was clearly distressing him.

"You didn't want to end up in the cholera hut," he replied. "The men in there were just skeletons waiting to die. Most were just too sick and weak to move. They were laid out side by side and they defecated through gaps in the bamboo floor. The RAMC [Royal Army Medical Corps] orderlies were wonderful. The stench [in the ward] was awful – how the orderlies stood it, I'll never know. They tried to keep the patients clean and comfortable until they died. But they never had much in the way of medicines or equipment. Sometimes they had to make brooms by tying grass on to the end of sticks to clean the shit up. It was bad alright."[10]

By July 1943, McManus was working from a camp called Hindato near a Thai village of the same name. At 5:00 pm on Tuesday, 20 July, he was admitted to the cholera hut, suffering from violent diarrhoea, vomiting, and abdominal cramps. Though he lived through the night, sadly, McManus died the following day. Then, like all the others, his body was hastily cremated outside the camp.[11]

After the war, in May 1946, the British government sent the balance of Gunner McManus's pay to his mother, Margaret. It was £100, 2 shillings, and 3 pence – a significant sum of money then. As his next of kin, Margaret could also have claimed his medals from the British government, awarded for the sacrifice he had made

10 Ibid
11 There is a slight dating discrepancy between the records of the Commonwealth War Graves Commission, and the Japanese camp administration. I have used the contemporary, Japanese POW records

for the cause of freedom. Of course, these things, though rightly given, are little compensation for a mother's grief. But the Irish government's action, three months later, was the political equivalent of spitting on a soldier's grave: They court-martialled a boy, long dead in the funeral pyres of the Burma Railway, in an act of callous spite designed to hurt his family.

And McManus was just one of many Irish Army deserters who fought in the Far East. James Oates, a 21-year-old labourer from Carrick-on-Shannon, served with the 1st Battalion Lancashire Fusiliers. He died in 1944, during the campaign to drive the Japanese Army out of Burma. Another deserter from the Irish Army, Patrick Reid, from Dublin, fought in the Burma campaign. He was a Gunner with 275 Battery, 33rd Anti-Tank Regiment. Patrick's older brother, Jimmy, also deserted and joined the British Army. Both men survived the war and were court-martialled together in 1945.

Patrick Reid died a few years ago. I spoke with his son, Paddy, and asked him how he felt about his father's actions during the war. Paddy simply said, "I feel proud."

Chapter 10

North Africa to Italy: Oiling the hinge of fate

Italian dictator Benito Mussolini launched an attack on Egypt in September 1940. Egypt, a former British protectorate, was defended by the British Army. Despite overwhelming numerical superiority, the campaign went badly for the Italians. And, by January 1941, Mussolini's troops were defeated and pushed back to their Libyan colony.

Hitler decided to bolster his ally's efforts by sending a German expeditionary force. The Afrika Korps landed with two tank divisions, led by General Erwin Rommel, a brilliant tactician who soon acquired the nickname "the desert fox". And for the next two and a half years, the Allied and Axis armies fought each other back and forth between Egypt and Libya.

Perhaps the most decisive, and famous, event of the North African campaign was the battle of El Alamein. For the first time in the war, Britain was truly on the offensive against Nazi Germany. It started in October 1942, with a massive artillery bombardment, followed through with an attack led by the armoured divisions of the 8th Army.

Two weeks of bloody attrition left the western desert ablaze with the smoking wrecks of brewed up tanks and the charred remains of their crews. But the Commonwealth forces had broken through the Axis minefields and driven the German Afrika Korps back into Libya. This, according to Winston Churchill, marked the turning of the "hinge of fate": "Before Alamein, we never had a victory. After Alamein we never had a defeat."[12]

But the hinge of fate was oiled with the blood of brave men. Victory came with a price, and an Allied cemetery contains the graves of over 7,000 Commonwealth servicemen who died at El Alamein. Britons, Americans, South Africans, New Zealanders, and Australians lie there side by side. Regardless of nationality, they fought for a common cause: freedom.

At least three Irish Army deserters died at El Alamein. James McKenna, a 24-year-old farm labourer from Scotstown, moved forward with the 1/7th Middlesex Regiment during the early hours of 24 October. They advanced through the German minefields under a heavy German artillery barrage. This took a heavy toll but failed to halt the advance. By the end of the day, the 1/7th battalion had fought its way up to the enemy Forward Defence Lines as planned. But the battalion suffered 20 men killed in action – including James McKenna.

12 The Second World War, Winston Churchill. Cassell & Co. Ltd 1959

Dundalk lorry driver Owen Mills died earlier in the campaign, with many of his comrades from the 5th Battalion of the East Yorkshire Regiment. And James McDaid, from Inver, a little seaside village in Donegal, was wounded on 26 October, serving with the 61st Light AA Regiment. The enemy captured him, and he died a few weeks later, whilst still a prisoner of war.

In November 1942, British, Commonwealth, and American forces landed in Algeria and Morocco. The Germans responded by sending troops from Sicily, who, initially, checked the Allied advance. Further south, the Axis forces defeated at El Alamein withdrew along the coast toward Tunisia, and the British Eighth Army pursued them. The final defeat of the German and Italian forces in North Africa was drawing to a conclusion.

Patrick McMahon, a farm labourer from County Limerick, had deserted from the Irish Army. Like many of his peers, he found a ready home in the British infantry, where the traditional fighting spirit of the Irish soldier was especially appreciated. He served with the 10th Battalion of the Rifle Brigade. They were a Territorial Army (reserve) battalion, which originally recruited from the Tower Hamlets area of London.

By January 1943, the Rifles were in the thick of the fighting, driving the Axis forces into northeast Tunisia; they were ready for the final offensive. On 2 January, the battalion moved to a new area west of Bou Arada. The men immediately dug in and prepared defensive positions.

Three days later, on 11 January, D Company (Rifles)

was ordered into action. They were supported by the tanks of the 17/21st Lancers. The Lancers were fighting with poorly-armoured Valentine tanks. These tanks were nicknamed "Tommy Cookers" because, when hit, they instantly burst into flames, incinerating the crews. Their task was to assault a German strong point on Two Tree Hill and clear the ridge of the enemy. The soldiers climbed up on the back of the tanks and took what shelter they could behind the turrets. Then the tanks moved forward, guns loaded, ready for first contact.

It wasn't long before the Germans opened up on the tanks with small arms. The infantrymen jumped down and started advancing up the base of the hill. The Afrika Korps soldiers, battle-hardened veterans of desert warfare, poured a withering hail of machine gun and rifle fire down the hill. Then they called up supporting fire from four-inch mortars. The Rifles were taking casualties as they advanced up the steep hill, and the company commander discontinued the attack and withdrew.

Twelve men from D Company were wounded, and four were killed. Rifleman Patrick McMahon died with them, and his body was buried nearby. After the war, his remains were removed to the Allied cemetery at Medjez-el-Bab. He was court-martialled, *in absentia*, in Dublin soon after.

James Brady, from Ballyjamesduff, Ireland, joined the 1st Battalion of the Irish Guards (a regiment in the British Army). The battalion had previously fought in 1940, in the unsuccessful struggle to defend neutral Norway from

German occupation. Now the soldiers were back in England, training and preparing for the next campaign.

On 28 February 1943, the Guards sailed from Greenock, Scotland, onboard the P&O liner Strathmore. Once at sea, the troops were told their destination: Algiers. Nine days later, they landed in Algiers docks and marched, unconcerned by the miserable rainy weather and the German air raid, to their camp at Sidi Moussa.

On 13 March, they embarked on another troopship and sailed to Bone. It was an eventful voyage. A German U-boat fired a torpedo at the ship. Luckily, the torpedo missed and the troopship arrived safely. Relieved to be ashore, the Guardsmen were taken to a camp, and Brady celebrated St. Patrick's Day, on the 17th, in appropriate style: The Guards, being an Irish regiment, were issued extra rations of beer and wine, plus chocolate, a wartime luxury. The following day, the regiment went into battle against the Germans. It was the first taste of action for many of the men. For some, it would be the last.

The Irish Guards, supported by the Scots Guards, attacked the elite Herman Goering Division at Medjez-el-Bab on 27 April. At 4:00 that afternoon, the battalion moved forward toward its objectives. The German artillery threw down a tremendous barrage and, as the Irish Guards advanced through a cornfield, they were hit by a hail of shrapnel. Dead and wounded men lay strewn across the cornfields, whilst the walking wounded limped back toward the Regimental Aid Post. Meanwhile, Brady, along with the rest of No. 4 Company, was pinned down under enemy fire in front of an olive grove. The other companies, 2 and 3, were fighting against German tanks and armoured cars in another olive grove.

The Irish Guards' commanding officer, Colonel Montagu-Douglas-Scott, decided to concentrate the attack on Hill 212 and called down a heavy artillery bombardment on it. At 7:00 p.m., the battalion, led by No. 1 Company, advanced up the hill with fixed bayonets. This was too much for the Germans, who withdrew. But it was a hard-won victory; over half the battalion had been killed or wounded.

No. 1 Company remained on Hill 212. Then 2 and 3 Companies occupied Hill 214. A saddle, held by No. 4 Company and Headquarters Company, linked the two hills. Brady and his mates dug slit-trenches in the hard stony ground of the saddle, knowing that a counterattack was inevitable. It was evening now, and the stretcher-bearers carried the wounded through the fading light down the hill and back to the line of the road.

After a sleepless night, the battalion stood to at 6:00 the next morning and waited for a dawn counterattack. The Germans brought up a full battle group, led by the 8th Panzer Regiment, with Tiger tanks. The heavily armoured Tigers, equipped with deadly 88mm guns, broke through on the low ground. Now the Irish Guards were surrounded.

The German tanks were forced back by the battalion's six-pounder anti-tank guns, plus heavy fire from supporting British artillery. Later that day, at around 3:00

p.m., German artillery opened up with a fierce bombardment. Then the German infantry stormed up Hill 214. Brady and his pals in No. 4 Company fired their .303 rifles and Bren Light Machine Guns downhill at the advancing Germans. Then No. 1 Company attacked from the flank, and the Germans broke and ran. At about 7:00 p.m., the Germans attacked Hill 214 again. And again, No. 4 Company took part in the counterattack, using rifles, grenades and even bayonets.

Whilst the infantry were fighting on the hill, Churchill tanks pushed the German armour back. Nonetheless, the situation was getting desperate. Supplies of food and, more importantly, water, were running low. But the Guardsmen's morale was high. Despite the heavy casualties and the loss of many of their officers, there was no question of surrender whilst they still had ammunition.

The following morning, 29 April, a supply detail from the Irish Guards broke through with some much-needed ammunition. This was just in time. German Panzer Grenadiers attacked on Hills 212 and 214 and along the ridge between them. Brady, along with the survivors of No. 4 Company, fought to hold the saddle joining the two hills. But sometime later that day, James Brady died of wounds sustained in the battle.

The Germans made repeated attacks on the Irish Guards' positions over the next 24 hours. But the Irish Guards held the hill until relieved, later in the day, by the Gordon Highlanders and the Grenadier Guards.

The 1st Battalion of the Irish Guards took the positions

assigned to them. They then held those positions in the face of overwhelming odds. They stood undaunted, with never a thought of surrender. By the time they were relieved, there were only 80 men left from the original force of over 400.

General Alexander, the Allied Commander-in-Chief, sent the following message to the surviving soldiers of the 1st Battalion of the Irish Guards: "Congratulations to you … for your magnificent fight which has … been of the utmost importance to the whole battle. I am immensely proud of you all."

Alexander went on to convey his sympathy for the battalion's losses, which, of course, included Brady. Two years later, the Irish government conveyed its feelings by posthumously court-martialling him.

James Brady's remains are interred in Massicault War Cemetery in Tunisia. He isn't the only Irish Army deserter to lie there. Patrick Conway, a labourer from County Limerick, is buried a few rows away from his countryman.

In 1943, Conway served with the 1st Battalion (1 Para) of the Parachute Regiment. 1 Para arrived in Algeria by train, on 11 January 1943. The battalion was crammed into cattle trucks, so everyone was glad when they arrived and marched to new billets on a farm. The next few days were spent training and preparing for the next operation. And Conway, like the other Catholics, was able to attend a Church Parade, or mass, on 17 January.

Aside from the odd ecclesiastical diversion, training continued until 22 January, when orders arrived, putting the battalion on two hours notice to move. The battalion sprang into feverish action, packing stores and preparing individual kit. Then, in a manner familiar to generations of soldiers the world over, they sat and waited for further orders.

Eventually, the paras went on to fight at Djebel Mansour and then in the Battle of El Mansour. For Conway's battalion, the end result of this engagement was 35 dead, 132 wounded, and 16 missing (dead or captured). *If* Conway had deserted the Irish Army for money, he was certainly earning it.

On 27 February, the Afrika Korps attacked and took the high ground in front of the battalion's positions on the Argoub. 1 Para launched a counter-attack and took 60 prisoners. The Germans responded with heavy mortar and artillery fire. A few days later, on 2 March 1943, Patrick Conway died of wounds sustained in the battle. It isn't clear exactly when Conway was wounded, though it was probably during the counterattack or the earlier German artillery barrage.

Many other deserters from the Irish Army took part in the battles to drive the fascists out of North Africa – men like Leonard Keating, from Tipperary, who joined the Royal Irish Fusiliers in 1939, and died with them at Medjez-el-Bab in 1943. These men died in some of the most decisive battles of World War II. If the Allied forces in North Africa had been defeated, the way would have been clear for the Nazis to take the Suez Canal and advance eastwards into Iraq and Saudi Arabia. And with

German strategic command of the Suez supply route, and control of the Middle East's rich oil reserves, World War II might have had a very different outcome.

★ ★ ★

After defeating the Germans in North Africa, the Allies turned their attention to Italy. On 3 September 1943, the Allies landed in Sicily for the first stage of the invasion of Italy. In the Soviet Union, the Nazi armies were slaughtering Russians by the millions. So the landings in Italy went some way to answer Soviet leader Joseph Stalin's demands to open a second front in Europe. It also served to draw German troops away from France, in preparation for the (real) second front to be opened the following year.

The morally and militarily pragmatic Italians, seeing the writing on the wall, abandoned fascism and discovered democracy. Benito Mussolini was strung up on a meat hook, and the country's erstwhile ally, Germany, abandoned. The new Italian government agreed an armistice with the Allies and re-entered the war on the Allied side. But Germany wasn't prepared to give up Italy without a fight. And the campaign to drive the Nazis out proved to be a long and bloody one.

Private John Dorman's part in the campaign would be bloody too – but short. Two years earlier, he'd been serving with the Irish Army. In June 1941, he deserted, travelled to Omagh, in Northern Ireland, and enlisted in the British

Army. After basic training, Dorman was posted to 79 Company (Pioneer Corps), and he served with them in North Africa.

On 8 September 1943, 79 Company embarked on LST 319, for the voyage from Tripoli to the beachhead at Salerno. The first serials from 79 Company landed on the beach, with the initial wave of assault troops, at 3:00 the following morning.

Dorman, along with the remainder of the Company, waded through the surf and was ashore by 9:30 a.m. It was a hot landing zone. The Italians had been disarmed and replaced by the German 16th Panzer Division, whose tanks were fighting on the beaches. German tank, rifle, machine gun, and artillery fire pounded the Pioneers as they came ashore, and accurate German mortar fire also inflicted heavy casualties. And, now that it was daylight, the *Luftwaffe* made its presence felt, too.

The Pioneers' task was to unload stores from the landing craft. But they were ready to fight as infantry when needed. No. 3 Section took heavy casualties and was almost wiped out. No. 4 Section, armed with Lee Enfield .303 rifles, assaulted a German pillbox (a fortified concrete gun emplacement). The occupants, unusually for the *Wehrmacht*, surrendered and were taken to the rear. Then 79 Company HQ moved forward and established itself about a mile inland from Salerno Bay. But heavy German rifle and machine gun fire hammered HQ's positions. So they withdrew slightly, to the northeast of the main axis of the advance.

On the beachhead, the *Luftwaffe* renewed its aerial attacks. The Pioneers dug themselves in, trying to take cover from the rain of artillery, mortar, and aerial bombs. But the bombardment took its toll, and John Dorman was killed. Like many of his comrades, he was buried in a temporary grave and later re-interred in the Commonwealth War Cemetery in Salerno. The remainder of 79 Company fought on for another 16 days, until the beachhead was finally assured.

The war in Italy continued, with the Germans being pushed back from a series of defensive lines. Each line was bloodily and stubbornly defended. Felix Carpenter, from Dublin, died in May 1944 at Monte Cassino, amidst some of the worst carnage of World War II. Maurice Cannon, a labourer from Donegal, was killed in action in June 1944, a few days after celebrating his 24th birthday. He died fighting with the 2nd Battalion King's Liverpool Regiment at Assisi. Three months later, Patrick Keane, from Rosbrien, was killed in action when the King's Regiment assaulted Coriano Ridge. But they wouldn't be the last Irish Army deserters to die in combat: The butcher's bill wasn't paid yet …

Chapter 11

Bomber Command: The Virtual Certainty of Death

Nicholas McNamara, from County Limerick, joined the Irish Army at the start of the Second World War. In September 1941, he deserted and went to England to join the RAF.

After basic recruit training, and possibly some time in a ground role, McNamara volunteered for aircrew selection with Bomber Command. For much of the war, only Bomber Command was able to hit the Nazis on their home ground and take the war to Germany. Night after night, they raided German military and industrial targets. They also played a more intangible, but equally valuable, role in maintaining morale on the home front. But the crews paid a heavy price for this: Aircrew losses were nearly 75 percent. According to Air Marshall Sir Arthur Harris, the head of Bomber Command, aircrews faced "the virtual certainty of death, probably in one of its least pleasant forms."

McNamara trained as an air gunner. It was the shortest

training course, and the most dangerous job in a bomber crew. McNamara finished his six-week gunnery course and was posted to an Operational Training Unit (OTU). This is where men "crewed up" – pilots, navigators, bomb aimers and gunners coming together and forming crews who would live, fly, and very likely die together. McNamara found himself serving with men from all over the Commonwealth. His pilot came from New Zealand. The navigator, bomb aimer, and mid-upper gunner were British. The rest of the crew came from Canada and Australia.

On 1 April 1944, McNamara's crew was posted to RAF station Little Staughton to form a new squadron. It was a damp, foggy morning. By midday, the visibility improved, and a flight of heavy Lancaster Bombers from 7 Squadron at RAF Oakington flew in. Another flight from 156 Squadron, at RAF Upton, landed and joined them. They formed up to become 852 (Pathfinder) Squadron. One of their pilots, South African Edwin Swales, was later posthumously awarded the Victoria Cross, Britain's highest award for bravery.

The Pathfinders were made up of the best bomber crews. They flew ahead of the main force, dropping target-marking (illuminating) bombs to guide the rest of the bombers to the target. In little over one year, 852 Squadron lost 35 aircraft and suffered over 135 aircrew deaths. They flew their last mission in May 1945, dropping food to starving Dutch civilians in newly liberated Holland.

But on 16 January 1945, the squadron's target was the

Braunkohle-Benzin factory, in Zeitz (central Germany), which made synthetic oil fuel. In 1944, German Armaments Minister Albert Speer had admitted that, with the saturation bombing of the fuel plants, the technological war was lost and soon the Third Reich would have no fuel production worth mentioning.

Of course, Sergeant McNamara knew nothing of Speers' pronouncements as he swaddled himself in extra layers of clothing, pulled his fur-lined flying boots over thick woollen socks, and went out to Lancaster NE130. This was the crew's 31st mission. Normally, bomber crews that completed 30 operational missions were transferred to training duties. This was to give them some hope of surviving to the end of the war. But McNamara was part of the elite Pathfinder force, and they served a tour of 40 missions before they were rested.

The morning started off damp and cloudy, with poor visibility. But by evening, the light drizzle stopped and the cloud base was up to 2,000 feet. It was good enough to fly. At 6:35 p.m., the light from a flare fired from the side of Control Tower announced take off.

When they were over the English Channel, the gunners went through the routine task of testing guns. The rear-gunner, sat in the isolated Plexiglas gun turret, was always cold. None of 852 Squadron's aircrew had suffered from frostbite this month, but in the unheated, draughty gun turrets of wartime bombers, flying at altitudes up to 23,000 feet, gunners sometimes did. However, McNamara had more than the cold to worry about.

Like his counterparts in hundreds of other bombers flying missions over Europe, McNamara constantly scanned the skies for signs of the deadly Junker 88 night-fighters. These fast, manoeuvrable, heavily armed fighters were guided in by German ground control radar, and they took a heavy toll on the much slower British bombers.

At around 10:00 p.m., the seven Lancaster pathfinders approached the target ahead of the main bomber force. They avoided the *Luftwaffe* night-fighters on the final leg and flew through heavy flak to the target. Below, searchlights were aimed up at the sky, trying to pick out the bombers for the benefit of the anti-aircraft guns and waiting night-fighters.

The Pathfinders dropped their illuminating flares over the target, but German anti-aircraft guns pumped a ferocious barrage into the sky. Shrapnel from exploding shells hit McNamara's aircraft, damaging the hydraulic system. The pilot, John McVerry, couldn't fully close the bomb doors. Worse still, the flaps on the trailing edge of the wings were damaged. This made the aircraft more difficult to control as it left the target.

Behind them, the main bomber force dropped their bombs, a mixture of high explosives and incendiaries. The oil-works erupted in a series of explosions, and bright orange flashes lit up the sky. Looking out of his gun turret, McNamara could see dense black smoke pouring out of the Zeitz plant as the Pathfinders headed back toward England.

Nine minutes later, a German night-fighter, probably

a Junkers 88, attacked Lancaster NE130. It was a cloudless night, with a covering of snow on the ground reflecting the ambient light. In the excellent visibility, the Lancaster stood out against the night sky. The Ju 88's preferred method of attack was to come in from the rear, flying behind and below, and fire a long burst from their canons into the belly of their victim. McNamara, who didn't see the fighter approaching, was immediately wounded, his gun turret destroyed. Meanwhile, a burst of fire raked down the complete length of the Lancaster's fuselage, shooting away the elevator control and damaging four of the fuel tanks.

The night-fighter broke off the attack and McVerry nursed the Lancaster onward, heading over France. It was clear to the crew that they were not going to make it home. Their only option was to bail out of the doomed aircraft. Two crew members pulled McNamara out of his gun turret. They grabbed his parachute from the rack, just inside the fuselage, and dragged him across the tail plane walkway to the rear door. Then they attached some line to the ripcord of McNamara's parachute and dropped him out the door in a desperate attempt to save his life before the aeroplane crashed. The line deployed the chute as McNamara fell through the air, and the canopy opened above him. McNamara landed on the ground but soon died of wounds sustained earlier during the night-fighter attack.

Sergeant Nicholas McNamara's reasons for deserting, travelling to England, and volunteering for RAF Bomber

Command lie buried with him. But knowing he had a far *worse* than 50 percent chance of dying, it seems difficult to imagine that he was tempted by a few extra shillings a day. He died gallantly and honourably, in the final stages of the war to liberate Europe. Seven months later, the government of Eire added his name to the List.

Chapter 12

D-Day: The Great Crusade

Joseph Mullaly from County Westmeath, John Hyland from Waterford, and John Keating from County Wexford lie together, amongst the 4,144 neat, well-tended graves, in Bayeux War Cemetery. A memorial records the names of another 1,800 soldiers, "known unto God," whose bodies were never found. They all died in the D-Day landings and during the subsequent fighting in Normandy.

There were Czechs, Poles, Frenchmen, Belgians, Norwegians, and many other nationalities fighting with the main British and American armies on D-Day. Most had escaped from occupied Europe, when the Nazi *Blitzkrieg* overran their homes. Then they'd joined the British Army or their own countries' forces (in exile). Their battle training was made as tough and realistic as possible. Live ammunition was used in training exercises; real grenades were thrown, and men died. But they were facing the *Wehrmacht*, the toughest army in the world. Its soldiers were a generation bred for war. From earliest childhood, as members of the Nazi Hitler Youth organisation, these men had been inculcated with a mix of discipline, aggression, and martial skills. Regardless of the ignoble cause for which they fought, they were simply the world's best soldiers.

On D-Day, 6 June 1944, the Allied invasion force lay assembled off the coast of Normandy. Overhead, 2,500 bombers flew deep into Nazi-occupied Europe, bombing rail junctions, bridges, and other strategic points, aiming to disrupt the flow of troops and weapons that would flood north to reinforce the German defences.

British and American airborne forces went in early to secure both flanks. Then, at 6:30 a.m., the first waves of men landed on the beaches. The US 7 Corps went ashore on Utah, establishing a bridgehead, whilst 5 Corps assaulted Omaha beach, where they were pinned down with heavy losses. On the eastern flank, British and Canadian soldiers of 1 Corps landed at Sword and Juno. At Gold beach, the 1st Battalion of the Hampshire Regiment (69th Infantry Brigade) spearheaded the assault at La Riviere. The 231st Infantry Brigade, which included the Green Howards, landed farther west near Le Hamel.

Like thousands of other Allied soldiers, the Green Howards had spent months preparing for D-Day. They boarded Landing Ships on 1 June, with a mixture of relief and trepidation. They were relieved that the waiting was finally over, but this was tempered by the knowledge that many of them were going to their deaths.

Because of the secrecy that surrounded every aspect of the D-Day planning, Joseph Mullally and his mates weren't to know that they would spend the next few days in the cramped confines of the ship. On 4 June, well-attended church services were held on all the ships. Then the ships set sail from Portsmouth. They passed out of the Solent toward the Needles (in the Isle of Wight) and immediately felt the effects of the bad weather, plunging around and making some men seasick. Then the ships turned back: D-Day had been postponed for 24 hours. The feelings of tension and anti-climax amongst the men must have been almost palpable.

Back at Allied Headquarters, Allied D-Day commander and future American president Dwight D. Eisenhower consulted with the meteorologists. Scottish RAF meteorologist J.M. Stagg forecasted a break in the weather for the following day. The consequences were potentially catastrophic if the landings went ahead and he was wrong. Strong winds and rough seas might have prevented many landing craft from getting onto the beach. Those that did make it ashore would have disembarked troops weakened and demoralised by seasickness. Airborne landings to silence German heavy gun positions would have had to be cancelled. The naval bombardment of German shore defences would have been inaccurate and ineffective. And the landings might well have failed, dramatically altering the course of World War II.

Against the advice of US weathermen, Eisenhower decided to go ahead. Fortunately, Stagg was correct in his prediction of a break in the bad weather. Meanwhile, unaware of the drama being played out at HQ, the Green Howards set sail again on 5 June. They spent the night sleeping in hammocks onboard the landing ships in the English Channel, and were woken at 3:00 a.m. on June 6. The men washed and shaved and checked their weapons and kit once again. Breakfast, including a tot of strong rum, was served by the ship's cooks at 4:00 a.m. Twenty minutes later, the soldiers started boarding the small landing craft that would take them ashore.

The plan was for the 7th Battalion of the Green Howards to follow the 6th Battalion onto the beach. Whilst the 6th was mopping up enemy beach defences, the 7th would advance through their positions to capture an enemy gun position near Ver-sur-Mer. But the plan, the big picture, was far from the thoughts of many of the soldiers as they approached the beach. The flat-bottomed landing craft wallowed unpleasantly, and many men vomited from seasickness. Ships further out at sea fired thunderous volleys of rockets overhead, whilst naval guns, aimed at targets on the coast, added to the mad cacophony of death.

As each landing craft hit the beach, the ramp in each bow was lowered. The troops raced out, thankful to be ashore again; one of them was Private Joseph Mullally. Nothing in his previous life, as a labourer in Westmeath, or as a soldier in the Irish Army, could have prepared him for the sight that lay before him. One of his pals described the scene.

"The beach was in a state of organised chaos with tanks, guns, jeeps, trucks, personnel carriers; in fact, every type of army vehicle. Some had been hit and knocked out. Some were on fire. The heather, or grass, just off the beach was burning and clouds of smoke prevented a view of what lay beyond. Wounded men, including some Germans, were sitting at the top of the beach, and stretcher-bearers were carrying others down to the boats from which we had landed."[13]

The 7th Bn had all landed by 8:00 a.m. A few mortar bombs from the German defences fell amongst the men, but without causing any casualties. The German defence here was lighter than had been expected, and the soldiers made their way past the brushfires north of the beach and onto the road to Ver-sur-Mer.

Ver-sur-Mer itself was undefended, and the nearby German gun battery was already out of action. C Company rounded up around 40 German stragglers and took them prisoner, and then moved on to join the rest of the battalion on Eastern Road. German snipers backed up by occasional bursts from machine guns, harassed the battalion to little effect. By now, the battalion was working (in effect) as part of a battle group, supported by tanks from the 4/7th Dragoon Guards and guns from the 86th Field Regiment, Royal Artillery.

The 7th Battalion continued its advance and came

13 Private Tateson. 7th Battalion, The Green Howards

under German fire. They suffered light casualties, but kept moving forward and took 40 German prisoners. The advance, and the fighting, continued throughout the day. Two companies continued toward Fresnay-le-Crotteur, till they came under fire from German machine guns and self-propelled guns (artillery). The German guns knocked out four of the Green Howards' supporting tanks, each of which exploded in an inferno of flame and smoke. None of the four-man crews escaped.

The remainder of the battalion, led by C Company, advanced toward Coulombs. They came under fire, then withdrew and consolidated for the night. But that didn't mean resting. Patrols went out to make contact with the enemy, and in the morning reports came in that German tanks were advancing toward the battalion. But this was no longer a concern to Joseph Mullally. At some stage, either at Fresnay or Coulombs, he was killed in action.

Further east, on Green Beach, on the morning of 6 June, John Keating waited onboard a landing ship with the men of the 1st Battalion of the Hampshire Regiment. He'd deserted from the Irish Army and joined the British Army soon after, in November 1943. This was his first day in action. And what a baptism of fire it was, storming the beaches of Normandy with the biggest invasion force the world had ever seen. We'll never know what was running through his mind that day, as he listened to the naval bombardment pounding the enemy positions on the beach. Did he regret deserting from the Irish Army? Did he wish he was home amongst the tranquil green lanes of County Wexford?

But there was little time for introspection when the landing craft beached. Despite the heavy bombardment, the Germans remained in position and poured a furious stream of fire onto the landing ground. Mines, laid on the narrow beach, also took their toll on the troops. Further inland, the Germans put down heavy fire from concealed machine gun positions. Despite all this, the Hampshire Regiment pushed the assault forward, inflicted heavy casualties on the Germans, and drove them from the beach.

During the next two weeks, the Hampshires were in the thick of the fighting against the German Panzer Lehr armoured division. Much of the fighting in Normandy took part in the *bocage*. The small, irregularly shaped fields, surrounded by thick hedges and criss-crossed by deep sunken lanes, were ideal cover for German snipers and Spandau machine gun teams waiting in ambush.

Private Gladman, one of the replacements for men killed in action, graphically described some of the scenes that he encountered on his way up to join the battalion.

There were many makeshift graves containing German soldiers. Their bayonets had been fixed to rifles and thrust through the bodies with helmets hanging above. Boots and other parts of the bodies were showing through the ground. Later on, we passed two British soldiers who had been killed lying in a crawling position. A Padre [priest] was there and he had placed a gas cape over their bodies … as we passed, the sunlight reflected on their boot studs and there were flies buzzing above. Somewhere, the relatives back home would soon be informed.[14]

On 14 June, the battalion went into Defence Routine and was then withdrawn into Divisional reserve for 48 hours. The soldiers had the chance to go into Bayeux for much-needed baths. But the respite, whilst welcomed, was short-lived. On 18 June, the battalion returned to action, ready for the following day's assault on the heavily defended town of Hottot. Lieutenant Blackmore commanded a platoon in A Company [Hamphires]. He described the attack in his diary.

The attack on Hottot started in pouring rain, which began before noon. The start line was neatly marked with white tape, and the enemy gave it (and us) a terrific plastering with his mortars. We pushed forward under a heavy barrage with our Brens fighting a staccato duel against the faster b-r-r-r-p of Jerry's Spandau's. In the din it was difficult at first to know which was his artillery and which was ours, but one soon realised where the 'receiving end' was when we reached a sunken lane, evidently well pin-pointed by the enemy.

14 R. Gladman. 1st Battalion, Hampshire Regiment. IWM

Several men in D Company (the leading formation) were also held up in this lane. But the place was decidedly too hot for comfort; so we climbed up the bank and dashed across the next field through a hail of mortar bombs and bullets, luckily without any casualties. We shoved over a lot more artillery than the enemy; he seemed to rely more on his mortars.

We got to close quarters with him at a farm. One of his Panther tanks came rumbling forward right up to our position, firing everything it had. With great presence of mind, one of our anti-tank gunners caught the Panther amid-ships, but not before it had managed to get one of our Shermans [tanks] belonging to the Sherwood Rangers, who were in support. Both caught fire, but the Sherman crew managed to get out all right. The 'brewed up' tanks, now well ablaze, began to attract heavy mortar fire, and although A Company were still supposed to be in reserve, we moved forward towards the farm where Major J. Littlejohns (commanding D Company) had set up his headquarters.

No sign of the rain stopping after ten hours. Everyone is tired and wet, but we have moved forward nearly a mile from La Senaudiere, with Hottot another thousand yards ahead.[15]

15 The Royal Hampshire Regiment 1918 – 1954, David Scott-Daniell. Copyright, The Royal Hampshire Regiment Trustees

The battalion took heavy casualties at Hottot: One of them was Private John Keating. John had only been in the [British] army for seven months. He hadn't made a will yet. Like most young men, he probably felt he'd live forever. But, on 19 June 1944, he died a brutal early death, just like many other young men that day. The following morning, the attack on Hottot continued.

The battalion fought through France, and then led the advance into Belgium. Four months after landing in Normandy, the 1st Battalion of the Hampshire Regiment marched into newly-liberated Brussels. To the inhabitants, free after four years of the horrors of Nazi occupation, every man of the Hampshire Regiment was a hero. The Belgians cheered themselves hoarse. Some wept with gratitude. And it's not in the least fanciful to believe that many said a prayer of thanks for the courage and self-sacrifice of the men who died giving them their freedom – men like "deserter" John Keating.

Many other Irish Army deserters died in Normandy. John Hyland, 6th Battalion, Duke of Wellington's Regiment, landed on the beaches of Normandy on 11 June. He was in action the following day. Less than a week later, he died of wounds sustained in combat. By 20 June, over 23 officers and 350 soldiers from his battalion had been killed or wounded. Many of the remainder were suffering from shell shock. The battalion was effectively finished as a combat unit and was withdrawn from action on 6 July –exactly one month after landing. But the Allied advance continued, and on 17 September, the first Allied troops crossed the German border at Aachen. The battle for Normandy was over.

Before the troops had left England, General Eisenhower issued an Order of the Day. He told them that D-Day would be a "Great Crusade … to bring about the destruction of the German war machine, the elimination of Nazi tyranny over the oppressed peoples of Europe, and security for ourselves in a free world."[16]

D-Day, and the battle for Normandy, was undoubtedly the most decisive battle (in the west) of World War II. It was the German Army's last real chance to tip the balance of the war in Hitler's favour. Arguably, it was only Allied air superiority that prevented this from happening. It was, to paraphrase the Duke of Wellington at Waterloo, a "damn close-run thing."

The *Wehrmacht* fought with savage ferocity in Normandy, with many units suffering close to 100 percent casualties. On the Allied side, some battalions suffered losses that equalled the worse days of the Somme, or any of the other bloodbaths synonymous with World War I. And deserters from the Irish Army gave their lives in this great crusade to liberate Europe. In reward, the Irish government dishonoured their memory by including them on the List.

16 Order of the Day: 6th June 1944. Supreme Headquarters Allied Expeditionary Force

Chapter 13

The Final Push

Groesbeek Military Cemetery lies about six miles to the southeast of Nijmegan, in Holland. It contains the bodies of 2,500 soldiers who died in the battles to liberate the Netherlands from Nazi Germany. Some of these men died nearby, in the initial fighting, as the Allies entered Holland. Some died later during Operation Market Garden, Montgomery's push to capture the bridges over the Rhine. And some were taken there for burial after being dug up from the numerous temporary burial sites scattered across southern Holland.

James Davis and Michael O'Donnell both deserted from the Irish Army and joined the 9th Battalion, the Cameronians (Scottish Rifles). They share the sad, but honourable, distinction of a grave at Groesbeek.

On the 27 November 1944, the Cameronians moved forward to Lottam, close behind the retreating Germans. Later that evening, the battalion commander, Lt. Colonel Bradford, called the company commanders into battalion

HQ for a briefing. He gave C Company orders to attack an enemy strongpoint at Kasteel the following day.

At first light, one platoon from C Company went out as planned and approached Kasteel. A Pioneer assault section, trained in mine clearance, went in support. Snipers worked their way around the right flank to give protecting fire. But, unknown to the platoon, they were under direct observation from the east bank of the river Maas. At 8:20 a.m., C Company started their attack. The Germans held their fire, allowing the platoon to get close to the moat and ditches dug around the buildings they were sheltering in. Then they opened up with Spandau machine guns, and put long bursts of raking fire into the attacking Cameronians. C Company lost 20 men in this operation, including 24-year-old Irish Army deserter James Davis, from County Tipperary.

Three months later, the Cameronians were in action during Operation Veritable. The aim was to break into Germany from the west, and destroy the enemy between the Rhine and the Maas. Part of the Cameronians' task was to capture Moyland Woods, a heavily defended area that had to be cleared before the advance could continue. At 9:00 a.m. on 15 February 1945, D Company advanced into the forest, heading toward a small hill, designated Knoll B. Immediately, German large calibre mortar and artillery shells rained down and caused heavy casualties. Then the wireless operator was hit and D Company lost communications with HQ. So Colonel Bradford sent out a patrol to make contact with D Company. The patrol returned at 11:00 a.m., with news that D Company was held up near the attack start line and being hammered by German artillery and Spandau machine gun fire. It was clear that D Company had no chance of advancing any further.

One platoon from A Company also joined in the attack. Tom Gore, a Private in the Cameronians, remembers the assault on the German positions.

"The enemy positions could be seen through the trees. The order was given to open fire; 'Rapid Fire!' Approximately 9 Bren guns, 50 rifles and 10 Sten guns added to the noise. There was no response from the enemy position. Shortly after we stopped firing, two of our Support Company carriers appeared, equipped with flame throwers. The carriers raced towards the enemy positions before the Germans had time to recover from our fire. The carriers opened fire, first with tracer bullets, then, as they got closer, the dreadful stream of flames, burning all in its path. The enemy ran from their positions, some of them aflame, to be shot down, mercifully …" [17]

Meanwhile, C Company went up to support D Company. Their instructions were simple – "to overcome the resistance and reach the objective." C Company arrived on the start line and pushed on another 200 yards through D Company's positions, until two Spandaus held them up. Eventually, tanks were brought up in support, but they became bogged down in soft ground and couldn't

17 Private papers, T.S. Gore, 9th Bn. The Cameronians

reach D Company. By then, the Germans had had enough and 26 soldiers surrendered. C Company finally reached the objective at 4:05 p.m. The Cameronians suffered heavy casualties that day. Amongst them was Michael O'Donnell, Irish Army deserter and farm labourer from Bruff.

Corporal Edward Browne, Military Medal, also lies in Groesbeek Military Cemetery. He died on 30 September 1944. Three months earlier, Cpl. Browne was in action with his regiment, the 2nd Battalion, the Royal Warwickshire Regiment, at Bas Le Perrier in France.

Browne's company came under heavy fire during the attack at Bas Le Perrier. So Browne took his Bren gun and ran toward the German Spandau, which was firing at his company. The Spandau was a belt-fed machine gun, capable of firing hundreds of rounds per minute. Undeterred by the Spandau's lethality, Browne charged it, followed by the second member of the two-man Bren gun team, who was armed with a Lee Enfield rifle. As he ran, Browne fired his Bren from the hip and emptied its 30-round magazine at the Germans. He killed one of the German Spandau gunners and wounded the other one, putting the machine gun out of action and undoubtedly saving the lives of many of his comrades.

Corporal Edward Browne was decorated for bravery. The citation states that he "displayed exceptional courage in taking on an enemy machine gun post". He was awarded the Military Medal. The citation is signed by another Irish soldier, Field Marshall Bernard

Montgomery. One year after Browne's death, the Irish government court-martialled him and added his name to the List.

PART III

Chapter 14

The Shamrock Benevolent Trust

Adolf Hitler's successor, Grand Admiral Karl Doenitz, signed the unconditional surrender on behalf of the Third Reich on 7 May 1945. The Japanese surrendered on 14 August. Britain erupted in a short-lived frenzy of relief and celebration, with speeches and street parties on every corner. The recently liberated countries of Europe shared in the joy, with the added fervour that came from having experienced the miseries of Nazi rule. Throughout Europe, millions of displaced persons and former slave labourers of the Nazi war industries began the long trek home. And in Britain, victory over fascism brought with it the problem of demobilising around five million servicemen and women.

The British Legion and other charitable bodies, such as the Army Benevolent Fund, were deeply concerned about the prospects in Ireland for discharged Irish soldiers returning from the British Armed Forces. They perceived the Irish government as, at best, indifferent to the soldiers' fate and, at worst, actively hostile. Within Eire, many people involved in the administration of local government and the allocation of jobs recognised this. Alderman John Fallon, at Sligo Corporation (Council), was in a position to see the unfair allocation of jobs on a daily basis. He was moved to comment publicly about the "victimisation of [Irish] ex-soldiers of the British Army who were unable to secure any work".

The British Legion made special efforts to help. This can be seen in the disproportionate allocation of funds: The population of Eire made up seven percent of the (geographic) British Isles, yet received 16 percent of the British Legion's total expenditure.

Retired British Army Captain Henry Harrison was concerned about the duplication of effort and (alleged) inefficiencies in allocating charitable funds. In 1945, he came up with a proposal to create one single unitary charitable administration. Its post-war aim would be to help returning servicemen find employment and settle back into civilian life, and to administer all charitable funds to ex-servicemen in Eire from a headquarters to be set up in Dublin. The Fund would be legally constituted as a charitable organisation, and be recognised, both in the UK and Eire, with the charitable funds topped up by funding from the British exchequer.

Captain Harrison also proposed that the British and Irish governments work together, with each appointing a nominee to sit on the board. Harrison wanted a UK government representative, because he was also seeking

UK government funding. The inclusion of an Irish government board member was aimed at making the Fund more palatable to Dublin. It was also intended as a further sop to the Taoiseach, Eamon De Valera, who had expressed a wish to have some degree of government control over the arrangements for the re-settlement of de-mobilised Irish members of the British Army.

Harrison took his proposals to Sir Eric Machtig, the Permanent Under-Secretary of the Dominions Office. It seems likely that Harrison had the backing of General Sir Hubert Gough, famous (or perhaps infamous) for his role in the Curragh mutiny: In 1914 he had told the War Office that he, and the officers under his command, would refuse to march north against the Ulster Volunteers, if ordered to, to enforce the Home Rule Act . And Gough, who was now President of the Commonwealth Irish Association, was influential enough to have Harrison's proposal taken seriously. So Machtig passed it to Sir John Maffey, the United Kingdom Representative in Eire, for comment.

Maffey, a politically experienced former colonial administrator, pointed out a number of problems (aside from his own reluctance to see formal Irish governmental control over the distribution of British funds). By changing the focus of charitable aid from unofficial bodies to an officially recognised organisation, aid would become politicised. The Irish government would be forced to formally adopt either a favourable or unfavourable attitude toward aiding a section of its populace *perceived* not to have fully accepted Irish nationalism and to favour anti-neutrality. Maffey felt that, "it would be a regimentation of those Irishmen who had not fully accepted the Nationalist ticket. It would be *represented* [emphasis added] as an enrolment of West Britons."

It was thought that, at best, the Irish government would refuse to nominate a representative. Or, if it did, it would be with the objective of sabotage from within. Also, association with General Gough and the Commonwealth Irish Association, neither well-regarded in nationalist circles, was only likely to deepen suspicions. Overall, Maffey felt that it would be in the ex-servicemen's best interests to continue with the unofficially recognised, and tolerated, work of the existing charitable bodies, whilst seeking to coordinate activities and make efficiencies.

But Maffey also clearly considered it to be the duty of the Dominions Office to formally champion the cause of the Irish ex-servicemen. And the office of the UK Representative in Eire put in repeated appeals, on behalf of *all* the Irish volunteers, to the Dominions Office in London. Maffey expressed his grave concern, about "… the Eire Government's generally unfriendly attitude to those Eire citizens who have served in our forces … particularly to ex-members of the Eire Defence Forces." But the Dominions Office was well aware of this. Their memorandum, "Regarding Certain Volunteers, From Eire, Now Serving With His Majesty's Forces", laid out some of the problems.

Of course, the term, 'certain volunteers' was a diplomatic nicety meaning the deserters from the Irish Army. These men had the option either to remain in Great

Britain or return to Ireland. If they chose to return to Ireland, their immediate difficulty would be gaining reinstatement in civilian employment.

Ireland was suffering from high unemployment, exacerbated by the return of thousands of civilian workers from the UK war industries and the demobilisation of the Irish Army. This was a milieu within which all the volunteers who fought against fascism suffered from official "prejudice against those who had left Eire to serve a foreign power". And the situation was exacerbated, for *certain* volunteers, by the stigma and discriminatory effect of inclusion on the List.

But there was little the UK government could do, to affect government policies, or economic realities, for ex-servicemen within Eire. The government would have liked to do something though. The ex-servicemen were seen as a much-needed stabilising and friendly element in Ireland, promoting a more positive public attitude toward the UK, which it was in the UK's interest to maintain. It's also clear that the UK government felt a strong debt of honour toward those Irish volunteers who, as wartime Prime Minister Winston Churchill said, had "hastened to the battlefront".

Nonetheless, the only issue the British government could influence that would affect the situation for ex-soldiers *within* Eire was demobilisation. Servicemen were discharged from the armed forces according to various factors, including length of service and marital status. There were millions of men and women in the British forces keen to return to civilian life. It was a sensitive issue. The authorities had to devise a system that both treated everyone fairly and, just as importantly, was perceived by the servicemen as such.

The British government recognised that giving priority early discharges to Irish volunteers would help them to compete for the rapidly diminishing pool of jobs in Ireland. But the volunteers from other neutral countries, such as Argentina, serving with the British forces, had already been refused early discharge. And it was thought that giving preferential discharges to Irish citizens would prove divisive and cause ill feeling amongst the troops. So the idea was initially shelved.

But British politicians and senior military officers continued lobbying the UK government, pointing out the special circumstances affecting the Irish volunteers. The government eventually caved in and put one measure in place, allowing priority release on compassionate grounds. For example, some students were released in time to resume studies at Trinity College, Dublin. Compassionate grounds also extended to "men in professional occupations, who would lose those jobs unless they were quickly released".

This helped a small percentage of Irish volunteers. But these were mostly professional men, who had joined the British forces directly, and who weren't deserters on the List: men like Sub-Lieutenant Mitchell, an Irish officer serving with the Royal Navy. His family owned Mitchell's Restaurant in Dublin, and he was needed to help his father run the business. And whilst there were a few medical students and lawyers and so on on the List, most were labourers and farm-workers rather than professionals and businessmen. So the compassionate discharge scheme was unlikely to help many men on the List.

Within the UK, the men on the List were given the same rights and benefits as discharged British nationals, as were all demobilised Irish volunteers. This had been debated within the UK government long before the war had ended. In 1944, the UK Representative in Eire made representations, on behalf of the Irish volunteers, to the Dominions Office in London, in anticipation of the end of the war. He was concerned about men being already discharged, such as those who failed aircrew training or who were wounded and disabled in combat. And as far back as 1942, the Ministry of Labour and the Ministry of National Insurance had considered the issue and expressed concerns.

It was decided that after the war, demobilised Irish volunteers would be allowed to settle in the UK, where they were entitled to dole payments and assistance with housing and resettlement, and so on. However, the UK government realised that many men would wish to return to their homes and families. It recognised "the individual suffering involved" in being unable to return home due to being discriminated against and denied employment. The UK government was especially concerned for the men on the List: "Even worse will be the position of the men, numbering some four thousand, who 'deserted' (sic) from the Eire forces to join the United Kingdom Forces during the war."

If these soldiers did go home to Ireland, they had the option to return to the UK at any time. Then they would receive unemployment benefit and help in finding work in the UK. But they were not able to collect their UK unemployment benefits whilst residing in Eire. Nor, because of their service abroad, were they eligible for benefits from the Irish government. There was a reciprocal agreement between the two countries with respect to health benefits, but attempts to reach agreement over Unemployment Insurance credits had foundered due to differences in opinion over payment rates, conditions of eligibility, and length of payments. Britain did not pay dole to workers moving to Ireland, nor did Ireland pay dole to workers moving to Britain.

So, Irish volunteers returning to Ireland lost their eligibility for benefits and dole from the UK. Politicians and members of the public alike criticised this and lobbied to allow unemployment credits to be transferred. They argued that discharged Irish soldiers should be made a special case. But critics missed the point – soldiers in the British Army, regardless of nationality, had no accumulated credits to transfer. Members of the British armed forces didn't actually pay tax and Unemployment Insurance contributions.[18] Nor did they have to pay for food and accommodation.

This was in recognition of the nature and difficulty of their job, and the relatively low wages compared to civilian employment. The 1935 Unemployment Insurance Act

18 Later to be termed National Insurance

(section 96) stated that members of the armed forces, on discharge, would be treated, for benefit purposes only, as if contributions had been paid during service; but benefits were only to be paid whilst resident in the United Kingdom.

So the de-mobilised Irish volunteers could either stay in the UK and claim dole, if they were unemployed, or return to their families in Eire and lose it. From the British Prime Minister downwards, there was widespread sympathy about this. The UK government felt that special concessions should be made for the Irish volunteers to receive dole in Ireland. However, proposals for this were eventually refused on the urgings of the Treasury. They were concerned that, if special concessions were given to the ex-servicemen, they would also have to be given to the large numbers of civilian workers returning to Eire, who had worked in (often) highly paid war industries. These civilian workers were not considered deserving of the same special treatment as the soldiers. But, more pertinently, the Treasury felt that it would just cost too much.

It's easy now to see this as the miserable bean counter mentality of the typical civil servant–and this view was certainly expressed at the time. But Great Britain had destroyed its economy fighting fascism and liberating Europe. The country quite literally stood on the brink of bankruptcy and economic collapse, and many tough decisions had to be made.

The Irish government faced its own demobilisation

problem, too, albeit on a smaller scale. Naturally, the government did its best to help men leaving the Irish Army, providing what the Army Chief of Staff, Lt-General Domhnall MacCionnaith, recognised as " ... generous gratuities ... given to soldiers in recognition for their services during the Emergency". The Minister of Defence also made personal efforts to secure jobs in other state services for ex-soldiers

Deserters, however, weren't so well treated. The Irish government court-martialled 4,983 Irish Army deserters, most of whom were men who had gone on to fight with the British Army. On 8 August 1945, they were tried and condemned, *en masse* and *in absentia*, contrary to all the laws of natural justice, without representation or right of reply. This didn't concern one of them too greatly, however: Joseph Kehoe, from Baltinglass in County Wicklow, died the same day due to an accident incurred during his work with the Royal Engineers, bringing food and supplies into post-war Germany.

Surviving deserters who later wished to return home were concerned about being arrested and imprisoned. Martin Walsh, who had deserted from the Irish Army to serve in the Royal Air Force, wrote a plaintive letter to the Irish government, a year after the war finished. It began:

> Sir, I would like to have my freedom in Eire, and not to be caged up like a bird when I go home to see my people. I wish to return home ... as a free Irish citizen once more without Detention or Punishment.

Walsh sought a written pass that would allow him to visit his family without being locked up.

> I would be pleased if you would send me a form of protection when I enter Eire protecting me from the Military personel (sic) and Police. I want to see my people urgently.

The Department of Foreign affairs wrote a clear, dispassionate, legalistic reply explaining the terms of Emergency Powers Order (No 362). The letter finished with, "The question of arresting such ex-soldiers on their return to Ireland after a period of absence from the State does not, therefore, arise." So Walsh was told, in other words, he would not be arrested. But the reply neglected any mention of the List. And the pedantically correct note reeks of governmental disdain, and a lack of concern, for the men who deserted and liberated Europe.

But there was a degree of concern for the deserters within the ranks of the opposition party, Fine Gael, and even from some members of Fianna Fáil. And, in October 1945, Fine Gael brought a motion to annul Emergency Power Order (362), 1945. The ostensible reason for the Order, which, amongst other things, brought the List into law, was to prevent deserters from obtaining any employment with state bodies or local authorities. This was considered a severe punishment at a time when most available jobs were in the public sector.

But the true rationale for Order 362 was more complex. In practice, it didn't apply to the deserters who'd remained in Ireland. Its real intention was to punish men for fighting with the British Army after they'd deserted. The Order, signed by the Taoiseach, Eamon De Valera himself, resulted in a predictably furious debate in the Dail. Fine Gael parliamentary leader Dr. Thomas F. O'Higgins made the comparison between the deserters who'd stayed in Ireland and those who had fought with the Allies. He compared the (often) negligible punishments given to deserters who remained within Ireland with the draconian punishments in military prisons given to men caught when returning on leave from the British Army.

Dr. O'Higgins also reminded the Dail that during the highly controlled wartime years – with an expanded police force and an environment wherein nobody could even buy an ounce of tea without a ration card – many deserters who had remained in Ireland were not even apprehended. "Yet," Dr. O'Higgins exclaimed, "through the machinery of the state," those deserters who had fought in Europe were "sentenced to absolute destitution and absolute starvation".

Later in the debate, Dr. O'Higgins praised the idealism and motivation of *all* the young men who had joined the Irish Army in the early years of the war, believing it to be the best way to defend their country. Others went off to work abroad in better paid civilian factory work, he said. But these men had joined the Army, believing that there was a real danger to the state. Then, after a couple of years, believing that the danger of invasion had passed, some of these men felt that "if the menace that threatened the country was to be met, the place to meet it was at a distance ... [in] the forces of other armies".

Continuing with the moral imperatives, Dr. O'Higgins reminded the Dail of the horrors of war that these men had faced. Though dismissed in some quarters as exaggerations, the awful realities of Nazism and the Holocaust were now well known to the public. O'Higgins made the argument that the deserters were fulfilling a higher moral duty, only "... to find themselves branded [on their return] ... as pariah dogs, as outcasts, as untouchables ... for the crime of going to assist other nations in what they believed was a fight for the survival of Christianity in Europe."

The debate continued in the usual hurly-burly of accusation and denial. Michael Moran, the Fianna Fáil TD, for Mayo South, claimed that the Order was not severe enough – though he did concede that it should apply "... irrespective of the army to which our soldiers deserted ... British, German or any other".

Of course, the number of Irishmen who served in the German army was miniscule, and they were not deserters from the Irish Army. Nonetheless, it raises an interesting point: No Irishmen who served in the German Army, broadcast Nazi propaganda from Berlin, or spied for Germany, were considered to have committed any crime. So they were not punished, as were the men who fought *against* Nazism.

Dr. O'Higgins (and others) again made the point that

the Order was discriminatory, that thousands of deserters who broke their solemn oath suffered absolutely no penalty at all. Even General Richard Mulcahy, a former Commander in Chief of the Irish Army and now a government minister, spoke against the Order. He objected to the imposition on the Army of a new disciplinary code for deserters, adding his disquiet about it being an Emergency Order made after the cessation of the emergency. He stated, "It is in conflict with the attitude of the Army authorities to desertion … in that it discriminates in the punishment that will have to be suffered by people who are not caught, who did not surrender, and people who were caught."

General Mulcahy was troubled most about the discriminatory aspects of the Order. He went on to complain of its differing treatment between Army officers and [enlisted] men, and the throwing aside of the ordinary military code of law, which allowed the authorities to take individual circumstances into account.

Predictably, the government maintained its position that the Order was justified and fair. When speaking for the government, Mr. Walsh was clearly amused at times by Dr. O'Higgins' rhetoric. He smiled when listening to O'Higgins describing the List as a "starvation Order … stimulated by malice, seething with hatred, [and] oozing with venom". Finally, and equally predictably, the Motion to Annul was defeated and Emergency Power Order 362 was upheld.

Chapter 15

Double Standards

It was the discrimination and double standards of the List that troubled many of its Irish critics. Officers who deserted from the Irish Army were not placed on the List at all, nor were soldiers who deserted but didn't join the British Army.

For example, Private Denis Doran, from New Ross, had joined the Irish Army in 1935. Doran was a trained soldier serving with the 6th Infantry Battalion when war broke out in 1939. He was, in other words, just the sort of experienced man the Irish Army wanted to retain. But in September 1941, he deserted and went to England to work in a safe occupation, as a civilian labourer for Messrs Humphries, a firm of building contractors. By Doran's own admission, he did this "to earn more money".

A little over a year later, Doran wrote to the Irish Department of External Affairs, professing a wish to return to duty with his regiment, and asked for help in obtaining the necessary travel authorisations. He left his job in England and was subsequently deported by the British authorities. Then he was arrested by the Garda after arriving on the Mail Boat at Dún Laoghaire, on 18 December 1942.

It is not known whether or not Doran ever returned to duty. The likelihood is that he was discharged from the services. But he was not placed on the List, and nor were others like him. This is in stark contrast to the men who fought with the Allies – men like Daniel O'Connell, a labourer from Cork.

In 1940, O'Connell answered the Irish government's call for volunteers and joined the Irish Army. In March 1941, he deserted, boarded a train to Belfast, and enlisted in the British Army. At this time, most of Europe was under Nazi occupation, and he joined the struggle when the war appeared to be going badly for the Allies. He left his wife and children knowing that, at best, he mightn't see them again for a long time.

O'Connell joined 832 Company, Pioneer Corps, in the British Army. He wasn't destined to be one of the millions of Allied battle casualties. He was discharged from the British Army for medical reasons in October 1941. Three years later, he died in St. Joseph's Hospital in Cork, mourned by his wife, Annie, and his children. But unlike deserters who returned to Ireland after working in well-paid civilian jobs, O'Connell's name was added to the List – a year after his death.

Michael Joyce and William Moore also deserted in

1941. But unlike O'Connell, and most of the others, they didn't join the British Army. Instead, they started their own little crusade, liberating honest people from their possessions: Not long after deserting, they were arrested on charges of breaking and entering. But they weren't put on the List. It seems that the Irish government saw burglary as a far less criminal act than joining Eisenhower's crusade to liberate Europe.

Apologists for the List will say that this apparent discrimination is simply a by-product of the List's criterion for desertion: O'Connell remained absent without leave for over 180 days, so his name had to be added to the List … But O'Connell was living openly back in Ireland. He could have been court-martialled and discharged from the Irish Army. That is what happened to deserters who *didn't* join the Allies.

It is inconceivable that O'Connell's presence in Ireland wasn't known to the government. There were strict border controls and monitoring of people entering the country. The Garda in Cork would have been looking for him in 1941, and would have quickly been made aware of his return. There was also food rationing in place, and O'Connell would have been issued with a ration card. And if that wasn't enough, his death was registered in a public hospital and announced in the newspapers.

O'Connell (and others) was treated differently to the deserters who hadn't served with the Allied forces. He was discriminated against after his death. His widow and little children had the stigma of having their family name added to the List. But did the Irish government deliberately do this?

The question of casualties had been raised numerous times. For instance, in 1943, Oliver J. Flanagan, TD for Laois-Offaly, tabled a written question to the Taoiseach in the Dail, asking "… if he [the Taoiseach] is in a position to state the number of Irish citizens that have joined the British armed forces since 1939 … and the numbers which have been reported as killed, wounded, or missing."

Flanagan was not to get his reply; the question was "ruled out of order" (in advance), by the Ceann Comhairle, Speaker of the Dail. But despite this lack of transparency, the government had, at least, some knowledge of Irish casualties. The British and Irish governments exchanged details about the deserters during the war (the RAF had been provided with Con Murphy's Irish Army service number and military unit, for instance). And the Irish government managed to keep deserters' families under sufficient surveillance to be able to imprison their children and claim their Family Allowance. Plus, all newspaper obituary notices of soldiers' deaths were monitored and censored.

However, there is no written evidence still in existence to conclusively prove that the Irish government deliberately added dead men's names to the List. But, at best, the government made little effort to prevent it happening. And at worst, it was a deliberate slur on the memory of dead men, and an attempt to humiliate and victimise their widows and families – some of the most vulnerable members of society. But, whether by act or omission, it was unpleasant, mean-spirited, and totally unnecessary.

Afterword

Some philosophies, like Nazism, are so foul that the only justifiable moral stance is defiant opposition. Irish political philosopher Edmund Burke's much quoted aphorism, that "all it takes for the triumph of evil is that good men do nothing," has never been more apposite than in the context of World War II. And by their actions, the Irishmen on the List agreed. Their moral stance was to stand up and be counted in the struggle against fascism and Nazism.

As I have admitted, it would be specious to suppose that *every* Irish Army deserter who joined the Allies did so for pure idealism. Perhaps, as the Irish government argued, there may have been some who were tempted by the pay in the British forces. But is it really credible to imagine that the men who joined the Royal Air Force and volunteered to be aircrew did so for a few extra shillings a day, knowing that they had a 75 percent chance of dying in action?

Of course, young men since time immemorial have gone to war for visceral reasons that they probably little understand themselves. As the famous 18th century essayist and moralist, Dr. Samuel Johnson, remarked, "Every man thinks meanly of himself for not having been a soldier". But it was more than bravado that persuaded the Irish Army deserters to remain in Britain once they'd seen the realities of war. Many could have returned to Ireland on leave, and stayed there, facing punishment but then remaining safe. Very few did so. Instead, these soldiers chose separation from their families and the safety of their homeland. They stuck to their duties and stormed the Nazi defences of Normandy, dying in the *bocage* country of northern France, where casualty rates for infantrymen rivalled any day of carnage in the trenches of World War I. And one could continue with such examples, ad infinitum, but the point has been made.

Few wars, viewed with the sanity of hindsight, have much moral justification. But World War II was unique in being a truly titanic struggle between good and evil. Europe, and perhaps the world, would be very different today had the forces of the Third Reich triumphed. Western liberal democracy, for all its myriad imperfections, seems a better choice than the Nazi philosophy of *lebensraum*, the concentration camp, and the gas chamber.

We owe our freedoms and democratic rights to the men and women who fought, and sometimes died, on the home front and the battlefields of World War II. The deserters from the Irish Army, who joined the Allied struggle, faced the horrors of the bloodiest war in mankind's bloodstained history. They have earned our respect and gratitude. They deserved better than the List.

Acknowledgments

A number of organisations and individuals generously assisted with the research for this book. These include Con Murphy, Gerry O'Neill, Phil Farrington, Kathy Ferguson, Paddy Reid, Paddy Keating, William Morrison, Captain Charles Gifford, Captain Derek Overend, Paddy Sutton, Samuel Walsh, Gerald Morgan, D.P. Cleary OBE, Colonel I.H. McCausland, Stuart Wheeler, Jenni Allcock, Jeremy Jenkins, and Paul Evans.

Thanks also to Norman Brown and the incomparable Royal Pioneer Corp archives; Barbara Geraghty and Masami Kimura for translating wartime Japanese documents; Beverly Hutchinson of the Ministry of Defence; Kate Swann of the National Army Museum; Charlotte Hughes of the National Archives, Kew, and Cpl C. E. Pease. I'm also grateful to The National Archives, Dublin, the Imperial War Museum, and the Military Archives at Cathal Brugha Barracks, Dublin.

Thanks to Susan Hunt for permission to quote from the memoirs of her father, Mr. R. Gladman; to Maureen Tateson for permission to quote from the memoirs of her husband, Mr. T. Tateson; Mr. Tom Gore for permission to quote from his memoirs; and Gill & Macmillan for permission to quote from *The Irish Gulag*.

I'm also very grateful to those people who helped me with their wartime recollections, but who prefer to remain anonymous.

Thank you to Wendy Bloomberg for her typing skills. And special thanks to Katie Gutierrez Painter for her first-rate editorial input.

And finally, thank you to *Chickpea*, Cotham Hill, Bristol, for providing great food and a really nice place for a writer to sit in and write.

A Few Deeds Short of a Hero

by Robert Widders

Robert Widders is the last man alive to have served in all three branches of the armed services; the Royal Navy, the Army and the RAF. *A Few Deeds Short of a Hero* tracks his life from childhood through naval service in the NATO rapid response Atlantic Squadron during the Cold War, through Army military manoeuvres in Germany and active service in RAF Field Hospitals during the Gulf War.

Through his life-long service and brief period AWOL, for which he served military imprisonment, he paints a colourful picture of both the boredom and tragedy of war. This is interspersed with the shenanigans of a young man sliding towards alcoholism, and a penchant for feats of physical endurance including running the Bahrain Marathon and expeditions to both the Sahara and Mount Everest. Robert Widders has emerged on the other side of conflict and a life shaped by the military as a balanced individual despite the trials of war. He maintains that his experiences have only made him stronger.

Reviews

Graphically charts the highs and lows, boredom and excitement, camaraderie and tragedy of military life.
Liverpool Post

Wonderfully self-deprecating.
Ryan Tubridy, the Tubridy Show, Radio 1 (Ireland)

Adventurous is an understatement when describing Robert Widders.
University of Birmingham, Alumni News

Robert Widders has a wonderful style of writing that makes the reader imagine that they are sat with Rob in the NAAFI having a chat, reminiscing and laughing over a pint.
Queen Alexandra's Royal Army Nursing Corps, on-line book reviews.

An insightful and good humoured look at life in the British military: Essential reading for anyone trying to understand the psyche of servicemen and women and why they need our support while serving and afterwards.
Amazon: Customer Discussions